Vincent Kiernan

FINDING AN ONLINE HIGH SCHOOL

Your guide to more than 4,500 high school courses offered over the Internet

Library of Congress Control Number: 2005933606

Publisher's Cataloging-in-Publication Data

Kiernan, Vincent John.
    Finding an online high school / by Vincent Kiernan.
    p. cm.
    Includes index.
    ISBN 0-9761868-3-7 (pbk)
        0-9761868-4-5 (PDF)

1. Distance education--Computer-assisted instruction. 2. High schools--Directories. 3.Internet in education. 4. Education, secondary--Computer-assisted instruction. I. Title.

LC5803 .K54 2005
373.133--dc22   2005933606

Printed in the United States of America

To Matthew, Terri, and Emily

Contents

Is an online high school for you?

Are you an athlete who spends lots of time on the road, away from a traditional classroom? Or a performer whose days are spent on stage or on a set? Or a beauty pageant contestant who spends much of the school year on tours? Did you have to drop out of school to help support your family? Are you a single parent who wasn't able to finish high school?

If you can say "yes" to any of these questions, you may be able to benefit from attending an online high school, full time or part time. But the list of potential online students includes far more than these. You might find it useful to take an online high school class, or attend online high school full time, if you are:

- a gifted student looking for an advanced placement course
- an average student looking for a course not offered at your local high school
- a homebound student with physical challenges
- a student in a rural school district
- a student in an inner-city school district
- a student who needs to retake a course that he or she failed or did poorly in
- a student who wants to take extra courses in order to graduate early
- a student looking for a specialized approach to education, like a particular religious denomination or attention to gifted students
- a homeschooled student looking for supplemental or advanced courses

You get the idea: online education can be a good idea for just about anyone. Another thing going for online courses is their diversity. They offer many choices for students to go beyond the traditional high school curriculum. The availability of these classes allows high schools to offer specialized instruction to students in subjects they ordinarily couldn't offer because too few students would be interested. Although every bricks-and-mortar high school offers English and biology classes, how many can afford to offer a course in astrophysics or Hebrew? Both of these subjects, and many more, can be studied online.

If you give online high school courses a try, you'll be in good company, as more and more students are trying distance education. About 222,000 students were enrolled in online public high school classes in the 2002–2003 school year, according to a study by the U.S. Department of Education. The students were divided roughly equally between urban, rural, and suburban school districts, but almost half of the students came from large school districts. According to the Distance Education and Training Council, at least 250,000 students take distance learning high school classes each year.

This book is designed to help students and their parents decide whether online learning is right for them and to help them sort through the many available options.

Are you ready for online learning?

Before we go any further, an important caveat: online learning is not for everyone. Some people prefer the give-and-take of a real-life classroom with flesh-and-blood teachers and students. Others worry that they'll find online study to be lonely and isolating, while another concern is that a student might easily fall behind in online studies.

So here are a few questions for students and parents to consider before proceeding with online study:

1.   Will you enjoy online learning?

Online learning has a different feel than face-to-face learning. In many ways, the instructor in an online course is more of a guide or mentor than a traditional lecturer or teacher. That is, the online instructor creates opportunities for students to learn and the resources that the students need to do so. The instructor is available as a mentor, coach, and cheerleader, but it remains the student's task to work through the class's material.

It's also common for online students to feel a bit disconnected from their teachers and classmates. That's not surprising, since the class never meets in an actual classroom or a single physical place. But for students who rely heavily on esprit de corps with fellow students, or for encouraging nods from the teacher in the front of the room, the online classroom experience can seem disappointing. To be sure, the best online teachers go to great lengths to counteract this problem. They provide frequent contact with students by e-mail, set up online chats, and promote team projects in which students work together.

Ask yourself whether you're ready for your teacher and classmates to be hundreds, if not thousands, of miles away.

2. Are you self-motivated?

Much more than most face-to-face classes, an online high school class places great demands on the student to be organized and to get work done. Since (in most online classes) there are no regular class meetings and students can work at their own pace, students can easily procrastinate. To be successful in an online class, students have to take charge of their own learning.

So honestly ask yourself: Are you a self-motivated learner, or do you require nudging and nagging from teachers and parents to get your class work completed? If you're not highly self-motivated, online study probably isn't for you.

3. Do you have the time for online learning?

A common misconception is that online courses are easier, and take less time, than their face-to-face versions. Actually, online study is very time consuming: you should expect to spend 10 to 15 hours, or more, each week for every online course you take. You should plan to leave time for reading course materials and textbooks, completing assignments, and interacting with your teacher and fellow students. A great thing about online classes is that you can usually choose when and where you'll spend those 10 to 15 hours, rather than having to be in a classroom following a fixed schedule dictated by someone else. But that 24/7 flexibility doesn't mean that you shouldn't plan to spend the time at all!

So consider your work and study schedule. Do you really have the time needed for online study? If your day already is jam-packed, either look for some ways to free up some time or delay your start of online learning until your time is more available.

4. How are your English language skills?

In face-to-face classrooms, much of the learning happens through the spoken word, when students listen to the teacher's lectures and engage in dialogue and discussions with the teacher. But in most online courses, almost all of the instruction happens in written form: the student reads Web pages or other instructional material selected by the instructor, submits written assignments via e-mail, and participates in chats that rely on typed messages.

This means that, to be a successful online learner, a high school student must be proficient in written English. If students struggle with reading course material and preparing assignments, they will have enormous difficulty in learning the course's material.

Honestly, are your English skills good enough to allow you to succeed in an online, independent-study environment?

5. Do you have reliable access to a computer and the Internet?

As an online high school student, your computer will be your classroom, textbook, and notebook, all rolled into one. As a result, it makes sense to have the right hardware and software for the job. It's best if your family has a computer for you to use, rather than your having to rely on a borrowed computer such as one in a public library. Make sure that the computer has enough memory to meet your school's requirements.

You also will want a reliable, and reasonably fast, Internet connection. For a few courses, such as those that rely largely on e-mail communications, a dial-up connection may be sufficient. But for courses that use sophisticated video or graphics, or that require you to be online for long periods of time, such as for chats, you may want to investigate a broadband Internet connection to your home. These connections are faster than dial-up connections, and they don't tie up your home's telephone line. Two options here are (1) cable Internet, in which Internet data are carried to your computer on the same coaxial cable that brings cable television programming to your television, and (2) a digital subscriber line, or DSL, which uses your existing telephone line but doesn't interfere with voice calls. Unfortunately, cable Internet and DSL are not available in all parts of the country.

Ask yourself: Do you have access to a computer that will be sufficient for online learning?

6. How are your computer skills?

Of course, it takes more than a computer to successfully study online. A student also must be comfortable enough with the computer to use it effectively. One needn't be a computer geek to succeed at online learning, but a certain amount of computer savvy is important. Do you know how to use a Web browser? Can you use word processing software such as Microsoft Word? Do you know how to find files on your hard disk? Can you install software? Do you know how to use chat or instant-messaging software? Depending on the online school that you use, you may need to accomplish all of these tasks. You won't be completely on your own; the school probably will have technical support available to help you work through problems. But it will help things greatly if you're comfortable with making your computer perform basic tasks.

So consider: Do you have the computer skills needed for online learning?

Questions to ask when selecting an online high school

Let's assume that, after working your way through the questions in the previous section, you're confident that online learning is for you. You have the time and self-motivation to succeed, you have access to the computer technology and computer skills that are needed, and you think that this mode of learning meshes well with your personality.

Now you're ready to look for an online high school that will serve your needs. This book includes detailed profiles of more than 100 online high schools, with information on their academic standards, the courses they offer, the tuition they charge, and other important bits of information. Browse through the listings, or use the indexes in the back of this book to identify some candidate high schools.

But before you sign up, ask some tough questions of any online school that you consider. These questions will help you determine if the school will meet your particular needs. Asking the questions before you start class may help you avoid disappointment or frustration down the road. Some of the questions pertain to enrolling for a single course, while others are oriented to full-time online enrollment. You should see red warning flags for any school that refuses to answer these questions or gives you answers that you consider evasive or incomplete.

1.   Who will the instructor be? What are his or her qualifications? Will there be more than one instructor?

Parents and students often ask these questions about teachers in bricks-and-mortar high schools but sometimes forget to ask them about online teachers. Your teacher's skills and qualifications are crucial in determining how much you learn from an online class and how much you enjoy the class. So don't be shy about checking into the teacher's background and training. Ask if the teacher meets state standards for teaching certification in the state in which the online high school is operated.

Many online high schools ask students to fill out a survey about their experiences. Schools generally do not post the results of these surveys on their Web sites, but you might ask about survey results for the instructor of any online course that you're considering.

2.   What will the course cover? Does it meet local/state/national standards?

Just as you can't judge a book by its cover, you also can't judge an online course by its title. "U.S. History" at your local high school may cover very different material than a course by the same name at an online school. (The same, of course, is true of the same course at two bricks-and-mortar high schools, but students don't usually have two of such schools to choose from.) Ask to see the syllabus for the course, which will lay out what the course will cover, what assignments or examinations will be required, and how grades will be computed.

If the school is affiliated with a religious denomination, be sure to check if there is a religious orientation to the course. For example, science courses at some church-affiliated schools emphasize the viewpoints of creationism or "intelligent design," a related perspective.

Many local school districts and states have standards for what a course should cover, and some academic groups provide national standards as well. If you're planning to transfer credits to a traditional high school or to earn a diploma in a particular state, it may be important to ensure that your online courses meet these standards.

3. How and when will I interact with the instructor or students?

Online courses use many different technologies, and you should find out whether you're comfortable with the technology used in any course that you're considering. Some courses, for example, rely largely on Web pages, textbooks, and e-mail between the student and teacher. In this arrangement, there are no lectures, and the student is responsible for reading and comprehending the information that the teacher provides. This approach might be fine for you, or, on the other hand, you might miss the interaction with a teacher and fellow students. (In fact, many educational researchers believe that students learn better in online courses that are highly interactive.) Other schools set up online chat rooms where all the students and teacher can talk together; this could be a problem if the chats are set up at specified times that aren't convenient for you. A few online high schools use even more sophisticated technology, such as tools for online conferencing and even live video; these too can provide for more and better interaction than what e-mail offers, but also can be a problem if you're interested in being able to work on your course work at night or on weekends.

4. Is the course self-paced? How long can I take to finish?

Online courses are organized in many different ways. In most, you can work at your own pace, completing lessons as quickly or as slowly as you wish. Often, you also can start a course at any time of the year. Online high schools have a lot going for them. One is convenience: in most cases, you can work on the course at any time, day or night. Your high school may require you to check in online regularly (for example, requiring you to post a message on a bulletin board at least once each week), but you still have lots of freedom as to when you complete the course work.

Also, most online high schools allow you to work on a course as quickly or as slowly as you need. If you find the material easy, you can finish in a short time and won't have to cool your heels while others catch up. If you find the material difficult, or if your schedule gets in the way of completing the course work, you can take the extra time that you may need. If this arrangement interests you, ask how long you have to complete the course and if extensions to that deadline are available.

A few other online courses have more structured deadlines. For example, some follow a traditional academic schedule, with courses starting in the fall and ending in the late spring. In these courses, work is scheduled so that students will complete their courses on time. If you have difficulty in setting your own work schedule, this arrangement might help you be more successful. But if you discover midyear that you want to start a new online course, a highly structured program would make you wait until the next academic session to start.

5. How will I be graded?

Online courses use many different ways to evaluate a student's performance and assign grades for the course. These include online quizzes, writing assignments, and lab reports. Make sure that you're comfortable with the evaluation method used in your course and that the evaluation method makes sense for the type of course that you're taking. For example, you would probably want to avoid a writing class that relied heavily on multiple-choice online quizzes.

6. Who actually provides the course?

Just because an online high school offers a particular course doesn't mean that the school actually developed the course or that it is taught by a teacher at that school. Many online schools offer at least some courses that are designed and even are taught by other institutions. But high schools do offer courses from for-profit companies as well. If you're interested in a particular course because of the institution that offers it, make sure that the institution is not simply repackaging someone else's course.

7. How many students are in the class?

This may seem a silly question—after all, it's not like the school has to worry about finding a classroom that's big enough for the class's enrollment!

But the question is a serious one. Teaching an online class is not easy—in fact, many instructors say that online teaching is more difficult, and more time consuming, than face-to-face teaching. If your online teacher is overburdened with too many students, he or she may not have the time and energy to give your work the attention it deserves.

8. How much does it cost?

Many public online high schools offer free or low-cost online instruction, at least to students in the institution's own state. (The geographical index in the back of this book will help you identify online schools from your state.) But even many online public high schools do charge tuition to part-time students, such as those who are taking one or two extra courses to supplement traditional courses.

Private online high schools do charge tuition, just as private bricks-and-mortar high schools do. Some offer financial aid or prepayment discounts.

Also consider costs beyond tuition. At some institutions you may have to purchase textbooks or lab supplies. And, of course, you have to have a computer and an Internet connection, for which the Internet service provider charges a monthly fee.

9. Will there be any away-from-the-keyboard activities?

Many online courses require students to complete activities away from the computer. A biology course, for example, could include lab experiments. Or a physical education class might require a student to follow a particular fitness regimen; the student then would submit a log of the exercises that he or she performed.

Even extracurricular activities aren't out of the question for online students. For example, student members of the National Honor Society at the University of Miami Online High School organized a community service project benefiting Ronald McDonald House facilities in five cities near the students' homes.

10. What kind of computer will I need?

Many of the institutions listed in this book offer specific recommendations or requirements for their students' computers, but the fact is that almost any late-model computer will suffice. Ask to be sure.

11. What kind of technical support does the school offer?

When distance education works properly, it's a dream. But when there are technical problems—such as a lost password or software that won't work—it becomes a nightmare, and you'll need someone to go to for help. Ask your online high school about the availability of technical support. How do you contact them? By phone? E-mail? How quickly do they respond? Are they available at night or on weekends, if you plan to do your course work then?

12. Is the school accredited?

One factor to consider in choosing an online high school is whether it's accredited. Accreditation is a controversial issue in distance education. Some believe strongly that accreditation is the gold standard for a high-quality distance education program, while others see accreditation as a roadblock thrown in the way of distance education by the traditional education establishment.

In short, accreditation is a seal of approval for a given school's programs. That is, whoever grants the accreditation is certifying that they have examined the school and concluded that it's up to snuff. An unaccredited institution can still be very good—many private high schools decide not to get accredited, because the process can be quite costly—but courses from an accredited institution are more likely to be transferable to another high school and be recognized by colleges you'll be applying to in a few years.

Still, accreditation can provide a valuable window into an institution, in part because the accrediting agency looks more closely at the institution than any student or parent could.

If you're planning to transfer your online credits to another institution, check with that second institution to make sure that they recognize the accreditation of your online high school. Similarly, if you know which colleges you'll be applying to, check with them to be sure that they'll accept the diploma from your online high school. Generally, you shouldn't have a problem on either count, but it's prudent to check up front.

Earning accreditation is a lengthy process, which explains why some newer online high schools are yet to be accredited. A school starts the accreditation process by selecting an accreditor, or accrediting agency, and submitting an application. The accrediting agency looks into the school and, based on the information in the school's application, may grant the school a provisional or temporary accreditation.

Then the accrediting agency sends a team of experts to the school to examine its operations. Usually, these teams include faculty members and administrators from institutions that already have accreditation from the agency.

If the school passes this examination, it may later be advanced to the stage of candidacy for accreditation. After an even longer period, during which the accrediting agency continues to monitor the school, the agency may finally grant accreditation to the school.

Schools rarely lose their accreditation. After the school is accredited, the accrediting agency from time to time sends an inspection team to make sure that continued accreditation is appropriate. (The Distance Education and Training Council, for example, reexamines an accredited institution every five years.) And if problems arise—financial improprieties, for example—the agency may place the institution on probationary accreditation.

The most important thing that accreditation tells you is that, in the accrediting agency's eyes, an institution's programs are legitimate and well run and meet a set of published standards.

But there are many caveats. One key point to take from the preceding timeline is that the accreditation process is lengthy. Although a given institution may be accredited today, that accreditation is based on information and inspections conducted years (perhaps many years) in the past. It may be outdated.

Also, the fact that an institution is accredited says little about what your own experience will be with that high school. An unaccredited institution may have some top-notch teachers and courses, whereas an accredited institution may be full of duds.

It's important to ask exactly what institution holds the accreditation. If an independent online high school is accredited, that accreditation is based on the high school's programs alone. But if the online high school is part of another organization, such as a bricks-and-mortar high school or a university, the online high school probably is relying on its parent organization's accreditation. You must decide how much that accreditation tells you about the online high school you're interested in.

Perhaps the most important question is to ask who has granted the accreditation to the school. Anyone can hand out accreditation; there are no legal restrictions on who can hand out accreditations. Indeed, some schools have formed their own accrediting organizations. And accreditation is a completely voluntary process; no one compels a high school to seek accreditation from one accrediting agency rather than from another accrediting agency.

This means that it's not enough to know that an online high school is accredited. You must also know who has done the accrediting! If the accreditor has low standards, then you should place little faith in its judgments about high schools.

Of course, it's probably impossible for you to evaluate the quality of an accrediting agency. But you don't have to, because the Council for Higher Education Accreditation (http://www.chea.org) does it for you. This nongovernmental body certifies accrediting agencies. Check their Web site to see if a high school's accrediting agency is listed. If the accreditor isn't listed, it may still be a legitimate accrediting body, but you may want to give the matter a second thought.

There is wide agreement, among CHEA and other institutions, about the high quality of certain accrediting bodies. If an online high school is accredited by one of them, you probably can accept the judgment without much concern. There are two main categories:

Regional accrediting agencies: These accredit high schools (and colleges) based on their geographical location. They are the Middle States Association of Colleges of Schools, the New England Association of Schools and Colleges, the North Central Association of Colleges and Schools, the Northwest Association of Schools and Colleges, the Southern

Association of Colleges and Schools, and the Western Association of Schools and Colleges.

National accrediting agencies: These accredit institutions anywhere in the United States. They have become more popular among some distance education providers because of the potential national reach of an online high school. Some educators believe they have lower standards than the regional agencies, but the U.S. Department of Education (among others) disagrees. Several such organizations accredit college programs, but the only CHEA-approved national agency for high school programs is the Distance Education and Training Council (http://www.detc.org).

Another national accrediting agency commonly used by online high schools is the Commission on International and Trans-Regional Accreditation (http://www.citaschools.org). CITA is not certified by the CHEA, but many think that its accreditation has value, because CITA was created by four regional accrediting agencies, each of which is CHEA accredited—the Middle States Association of Colleges and Schools, the Southern Association of Colleges and Schools, the Western Association of Schools and Colleges, and the North Central Association of Colleges and Schools—and the National Council for Private Schools Accreditation.

13. Who runs the school?

Online high schools come in many flavors. Some are operated by public school districts and may charge little or no tuition to state residents. Others are charter schools, or publicly funded schools that operate separately from the public school district by a group of interested individuals; these too are frequently free to state residents.

There also are private online high schools. Some of these have a religious orientation. Others don't. A few online high schools are operated by universities as part of their efforts to help the community.

Some words of cyber advice

You are investing lots of time and money in your online study. Unfortunately, any number of technical problems can destroy that work— a lightning strike to the power line that supplies your computer, an attack by a virus that makes your hard disk unreadable, or even an editing error on your own part. As a result, you should consider taking some simple steps that can help prevent problems from happening and help you cope with them if they do. Many of these steps are aimed at users of the very popular Microsoft Windows, but some of the steps apply to Macintosh users too.

Antivirus software

Obtain, and use, antivirus software on your computer. It can be a heartbreaking experience to discover that your computer—and perhaps your backed-up files as well—have been corrupted by a virus or worm. And simply installing the software is not sufficient. Because new viruses and worms are constantly appearing, it's vital that you periodically update your computer's database of antivirus information. Follow the instructions in your antivirus program or preferably configure it to automatically update itself periodically.

Firewalls

It's likewise important to use a firewall to shield your computer from hacking attacks. Recent versions of Microsoft Windows have basic firewalls that will provide a sufficient degree of protection—but you must first activate the firewall. Unfortunately, sometimes a firewall will interfere with legitimate online education programs, so if you run into any problems, be sure to consult with your institution.

Windows updates

A third way to help make sure that a Windows-based computer is not derailed by a hacker attack is to keep your computer's copy of Windows up to date. Microsoft periodically issues patches aimed at correcting weaknesses in Windows that can be exploited by hackers. By downloading and installing these patches, you can improve your computer's security. To check for patches for your machine, visit http://windowsupdate. microsoft.com.

Software updates

You can strengthen your computer by downloading any patches for the software you run on it, particularly Microsoft Word. These patches include fixes for bugs in the software and for vulnerabilities that can be exploited by viruses and worms. For Microsoft patches, check http://office.microsoft.com/officeupdate.

Back up frequently

If you store your high school work on your computer, you should back up those files on a regular basis. Backups give you a fallback position if a file becomes corrupted by a software or hardware problem, and they also can be useful to consult if you change your mind about a new version of your writing. If your computer can write CDs or DVDs, you can make backups on them. If your files are small, they may fit on a floppy disk.

Institutional Profiles

T his section contains thumbnail sketches of more than 100 online high school programs operating in the United States. There is a broad range of institutions—public and private, secular and religious, large and small. I excluded public online high schools that do not admit students from outside their school districts' boundaries.

The information for the profiles came from the institutions' Web sites and from the institutions themselves. I include contact information for the institution (address, phone, fax, Web site, and e-mail), a brief description of the institution and the criteria for enrolling, and a list of the online courses that the institution offers. Then I report whether a student can earn a diploma online, how much tuition costs, and what, if any, specific requirements for computers are set out for online students. Finally, the profiles indicate what accrediting bodies, if any, have accredited the online high school.

Of course, online high schools are constantly evolving, so double-check any information before relying on it.

3D Learn

27499 Riverview Center Boulevard, Suite 25-A
Bonita Springs, FL 34134

Phone: Toll-free (866) 463-9138

Fax: (215) 754-4356

Web site: http://www.3dlearn.com

E-mail: information@3dlearn.com

Description: Welcome to 3DLearn, accredited 3D virtual reality distance learning and homeschooling for grades 7–12. What if you could get up in the morning and "walk" inside a 3D school, assume a visual representation of yourself. and then go "into" your classroom? What if you could create your own 3D objects, add books, papers, and even customize your own school desk? What if you could create your own exciting 3D worlds to go with your studies? This is not a "what if" with us! This is the reality of 3DLearn, so come join the fun and learn like never before.

Eligibility: Anyone may enroll.

Online high school courses offered:

3D Programming 1

Algebra 1

Algebra 2

American Literature

Ancient History

Art History

Basic Art

Biology

Contemporary Authors

Contemporary Issues: World Powers

Criminal Justice

Earth Science

English 1

English Literature

Environmental Science

European History and English: Double Credit Course

Fantasy Writing

Geometry

Introductory Chemistry

Journalism Studies

Physical Science

Problems of Democracy

SAT Test Prep

Senior Studies

Spanish 1

World History 2

Offers diploma? Yes

Tuition: $2,600 annually, or $350 per course

Computer requirements:

Pentium II CPU 300 MHz or equivalent

64 MB RAM

Microsoft Windows 98, ME, 2000, or XP

DirectX 8.1 or later

Windows Media Player 6.4 or later

D3D video card with at least 8 MB and the latest drivers

Accreditation: National Private Schools Accrediting Alliance

Abaetern Academy

1627 W. Main Street, No.376
Bozeman, MT 59715-4011

Phone: (406) 920-1778
Fax: (406) 585-2766

Web site: http://www.abaetern.com

E-mail: ivymerriot@abaetern.com

Description: The word *abaetern* means "before antiquity." This invokes the idea that even before recorded history, our ancestors craved knowledge and understanding in order to enjoy healthy relationships with their environment and each other. The name *Abaetern* symbolizes the idea that education is a natural process fundamental to the human experience. Abaetern's courses use the Internet as a tool to bring outstanding teachers and resources to students; each student, regardless of geographical location, may now gain access to the future he or she desires. Growing up in a rural setting is no longer a barrier to fulfilling our dreams! Abaetern Academy has created an efficient, yet personalized, learning environment: our teachers are facilitators, not lecturers. The students' own interests guide their activities as our state-certified teachers facilitate the growth of concepts and skills in alignment with national, state, and cultural education standards. This type of supportive environment causes the embers of our students' natural curiosity to ignite, resulting in the rediscovery of the joy of learning known to our ancient ancestors.

Eligibility: Anyone may enroll.

Online high school courses offered:

Acoustics

Active Galactic Nuclei

Algebra

Algebra II

The Anasazi

Ancient Astronomy

Ancient Cultures of the World

Astronomy

Black Holes

Buffalo

Calculus

Comparative Literature

Composition

Conceptual Physics

Creative Writing

Current Events

Einstein's Relativity Theories

Electricity and Magnetism

Exploring Mars

Fiction

French

Friendship

Gravity and Relativity

Identity

Japanese

Light and Color

Lodge of the Plains People

Math in Our Everyday World

Motion and Forces

Multiple Intelligences

The Night Sky

Particle Physics

Physics

continued on next page

Abaetern Academy
continued from previous page

Poetry

Seasons

Spanish

The Sun

Technology Warm-Up

Thermodynamics

U.S. Government

U.S. History

Water and Sky

World Culture

The World Today

Offers diploma? Yes

Tuition: $217 per quarter

Computer requirements: Computer connected to the Internet

Accreditation: Working toward accreditation from the National Association of Independent Schools

Alabama Online High School

The University of Alabama
College of Continuing Studies
Alabama Online High School
Box 870388
Tuscaloosa, AL 35487-0388

Phone: (205) 348-2647

Fax: (205) 348-2585

Web site: http://www.aohs.state.al.us

E-mail: aohs@ccs.ua.edu

Description: Since January 2000, the Alabama Online High School has offered Web-based courses that bridge the barriers of time and distance and create unprecedented opportunities for schools to achieve access, excellence, and equity in education.

Eligibility: Alabama residents may enroll through their local schools.

Online high school courses offered:

Algebra I

Biology

Career Tech Coordinated Studies

Career Tech Education Core

Chemistry

Creative Writing

Economics

English 9

English 10

English 11

English 12

Environmental Science

Geometry

Health Education

Physical Science

Physics

Spanish I

Spanish II

U.S. Government

U.S. History 1900–Present

Offers diploma? No

Tuition: The student's local school district is billed.

Accreditation: Commission on International and Trans-Regional Accreditation

Southern Association of Colleges and Schools

Alpha Omega Academy

300 N. McKemy Avenue
Chandler, AZ 85226

Phone: Toll-free (800) 682-7396 or
(602) 438-2717

Fax: (480) 893-6112

Web site: http://www.aoacademy.com

E-mail: academy@aop.com

Description: Alpha Omega Academy
offers courses for elementary and high
school students with an emphasis on
individualized learning. Online
courses, using CD-ROMs, are available
for grades 3–12.

Eligibility: Anyone may enroll.

Online high school courses offered:

Advanced Language Arts

Algebra I

Algebra II

Biology

Chemistry

Communication Skills and Literature

Foundations of Language Arts

Geometry I

Government and Economics

Health

Physical Science

Physics

Precalculus

Social Studies/Geography

Spanish I

Spanish II

Structure of Grammar and Genres of
Literature

U.S. History

World History

Offers diploma? Yes

Tuition: $1,100 annually, or $137 to
$275 per course

Computer requirements: Windows-
based computer, CD-ROM, Internet
connection

Accreditation: Commission on
International and Trans-Regional
Accreditation

North Central Association
Commission on Accreditation and
School Improvement

American Virtual High School

6750 Pembroke Road
Hollywood, FL 33028

Phone: (954) 964-7100

Web site: http://
www.americanvirtualhighschool.us

E-mail: admissions@
americanvirtualhighschool.us

Description: Study for your high
school diploma from anywhere in the
world through distance learning
online at American Virtual High
School. Graduates receive a traditional
high school diploma and official
transcripts, based on the American
system of secondary education. We are
a distance learning high school that is
committed to offering an opportunity
for quality education that is accessible
to students any time, any place.
American Virtual High School is a
private high school based out of Ft.
Lauderdale, Florida.

Eligibility: Anyone may enroll.

continued on next page

American Virtual High School
continued from previous page

Online high school courses offered:
Algebra 1
Algebra 2
American Government
American History
Anatomy/Physiology
Art
Basic English Grammar
Calculus
Career Planning
Chemistry
Child Care Management
Earth Science
Economics
English 9th Grade
English 10th Grade
English 11th Grade
English 12th Grade
English as a Second Language
English Writing
French 1
Geology
Geometry
Hebrew 1
Introduction to Biology
Introduction to Business
Introduction to Computers
Introduction to the Internet
Music
Physics
Practical Math
Prealgebra

Psychology
Sociology
Spanish 1
Spanish 2
Speech
Stress Management
Trigonometry
World Geography
Zoology

Offers diploma? Yes

Tuition: $250 per course

Computer requirements: A standard PC running Microsoft Windows with Microsoft Office.

Accreditation: National Private Schools Accreditation Alliance

Babbage Net School

P.O. Box 517
Port Jefferson, NY 11777

Phone: (631) 642-2029

Fax: (631) 642-2029

Web site:
http://www.babbagenetschool.com

E-mail:
babbage@babbagenetschool.com

Description: The Babbage Net School is a virtual high school offering online, interactive courses in English, math, science, social studies, SAT, foreign language, Advanced Placement, music, and art. These courses are taught by certified teachers in a virtual classroom featuring interactive audio, synchronized Web browsing, and a shared whiteboard. Tutoring and GED programs are available.

Eligibility: Anyone may enroll.

Online high school courses offered:

Algebra 1

Algebra 2

American Government

American History

Art and Music Appreciation

Biology

Biology Lab

Business Law

Chemistry

Civics

Consumer Math

Creative Writing

Earth Science

Economics

English 1

English 2

English 3

English 4

Environmental Science

Fine Art

French I

Geography

Geometry

German I

Grammar and Composition

Health

Introduction to Computer Technology

Introduction to Technology

Life Science

Lifetime Fitness

Marketing

MS Office Applications, Level 1

Physical Science

Physics

Prealgebra

Precalculus

Psychology

Refresher Math

Skills for Success

Sociology

Spanish 1

Spanish 2

Trigonometry

World History

Offers diploma? No

Tuition: $390 per course

Computer requirements:

Intel Pentium 150

32 MB RAM

Internet connection with 28.8-K modem

16-bit full-duplex Sound Blaster-compatible sound card with support for DirectX 6

Microphone and headphones

Monitor supporting 800 x 600 resolution, 256 colors or better

Accreditation: Distance Education and Training Council

Northwest Association of Accredited Schools

Basehor-Linwood Virtual School

2108 N. 155th Street
P.O. Box 251
Basehor, KS 66007-0251

Phone: (913) 724-1727 or
(913) 724-3131

Fax: (913) 724-4518

Web site: http://vcs.usd458.k12.ks.us

E-mail:
Brenda_degroot@mail.usd458.
k12.ks.us

Description: The Basehor-Linwood Unified School District #458 offers a variety of educational opportunities. The Distance Learning Program has been created for those students who are looking for enrichment opportunities and students who are seeking alternative ways of earning academic credit. All can participate in this exciting educational opportunity. If you are seeking academic credit, your local high school must preapprove each course prior to enrollment.

Eligibility: The Basehor-Linwood Virtual School is open to Kansas homeschooled students and students transferring from Kansas public schools. The Basehor-Linwood Distance Learning Program is open to all.

Online high school courses offered:

Algebra I

Algebra II

Applied Foundations

Biology

Business Consumer Math

Business Law

Child Care

Computer Applications I

Computer Applications II

Contemporary Issues

Earth Science

English I

English II

English III

English IV (Senior English)

Food Facts and Fitness

Geometry

Health

High School Reading

Independent Living

Introduction to Art

Introduction to Business

Keyboarding I

Keyboarding II

Physical Education

Physical Science

Prealgebra

Psychology

Sociology

U.S. Government

U.S. History

World History

Offers diploma? Yes

Tuition: None for Kansas residents in Basehor-Linwood Virtual School, or $300 per course in the Basehor-Linwood Distance Learning Program.

Blueprint Education

1717 W. Northern Avenue, Suite 104
Phoenix, AZ 85021
Phone: Toll-free (800) 426-4952
Fax: (602) 943-9700
Web site:
http://www.blueprinteducation.org
E-mail: email@blueprinteducation.org
Description: Blueprint Education, an international learning organization serving nontraditional needs, offers a wide variety of courses. Students may opt to enroll in one or two courses to either recover credits or to graduate early. Blueprint Education also grants a standard or college prep high school diploma for those students who choose a nontraditional school setting. Blueprint Education offers more than 220 courses in core curriculum and electives. Each course is designed and taught by state-certified teachers or university professors. Students work independently at their own pace without daily teacher contact; however, students may e-mail instructors at any time. Students may enroll at any time through an open entry/open exit system.
Eligibility: Anyone may enroll.
Online high school courses offered:
Accounting
Algebra
American Government
American History
American/Arizona Government
American/Arizona History
Automotive Essentials
Biology

Business Law
Business Mathematics
Calculus
Chemistry
Computer Applications
Computer Literacy
Consumer Mathematics
Contemporary English
The Developing Child
Diversified Work Experience
Drawing and Visual Perception
Driver Safety Education
Earth Science
Economics
Elementary Psychology
English
English Composition
Environmental Science
General Business
General Mathematics
General Science
Geometry
Health Education
The History of Ancient Art
Independent Travel Study
Intermediate Drawing and Painting
Interpersonal Relations
Life Management
Marketing
Music Theory
Parenting
Physical Education
Physical Fitness
Prealgebra
Religions of the World

Salesmanship

Self-Awareness

Short Stories

Single Survival

Spanish

Speech

Statistics

Study SkillsToday's Teen

Trigonometry

Weight Training

World Geography

World Geography/History

World History

Your Employment Success

Offers diploma? Yes

Tuition: $125 per half credit hour

Accreditation: Commission on International and Trans-Regional Accreditation

North Central Association of Colleges and Schools

Center for Talent Development

School of Education and Social Policy
Northwestern University
617 Dartmouth Place
Evanston, IL 60208-4175

Phone: (847) 491-3782

Fax: (847) 467-4283

Web site:
http://www.ctd.northwestern.edu

E-mail: ctd@northwestern.edu

Description: The Center for Talent Development's LearningLinks Distance Learning Programs offer academically talented students the opportunity to take enrichment, high school honors,

and Advanced Placement courses. These programs are designed for independent students who wish to move quickly to advanced levels of course work, whose local school offerings are limited, who have scheduling difficulties, or who are homeschooled.

Program offers fall, winter, and summer terms. Fall- and winter-term courses last nine months. Courses are Web-based and are not self-paced.

Eligibility: Program is aimed at gifted students; students must submit a minimum SAT or ACT score to qualify for admission.

Online high school courses offered:

A.P. Biology

A.P. Calculus AB

A.P. Calculus BC

Ancient Greek I Honors

Biology Honors

Chemistry Honors

Creative Writing Honors

Critical Thinking Honors: Informal Logic

Critical Thinking Honors: Mass Media

Dramatic Script Writing Honors

Economics Honors

English Vocabulary I: An Etymological Approach

English Vocabulary II Honors

Geometry Honors

Introduction to Philosophy Honors

Java Honors

Journalistic Writing Honors

Latin I Honors

Latin II Honors

Latin III Honors

Literary Analysis Honors

Math and Computers Honors

Musical Theater Honors

Nonfiction Writing Honors

Physics Honors

Precalculus Honors

Psychology Honors

U.S. History Honors

World Perspectives Honors

Offers diploma? No

Tuition: $550 per course. Financial aid is available.

Accreditation: North Central Association of Colleges and Schools

Central Connecticut Adventist Virtual School

86 Pebblebrook Road
Windsor, CT 06095

Phone: (860) 667-1669

Web site: http://www.adventist-home-school.com

E-mail: ccavs@adventist-home-school.com

Description: Our mission is to set the standard in online Adventist Christian education by harnessing the power of the Internet to extend the classroom beyond the boundaries of geography. Our goal is to provide students with an interactive learning experience that will challenge them intellectually and spiritually and point them to the Source of all wisdom and knowledge, Jesus Christ. Offers grades 4–10. Classes start in September and conclude in June. Students are expected to attend class during regular class times.

Eligibility: Anyone may enroll.

Online high school courses offered:

Algebra I

Algebra II

Basic Keyboard

Bible I

Bible II

Biology

Earth Science

English I

English II

Health

Physical Education

Spanish

World History

Offers diploma? No

Tuition: $2,390 per year

Choice 2000 Online High School

11 S. D Street
Perris, CA 92570

Phone: (951) 940-5700

Web site: http://www.choice2000.org

E-mail: swenzel@puhsd.org

Description: Choice 2000 is proud to offer students cutting-edge technologies to complete their high school course work entirely over the Internet. This includes a live online virtual classroom environment, the ability to receive and turn in homework assignments online, as well as a secure online assessment environment. Classes run from August

continued on next page

Choice 2000 Online High School
continued from previous page

to June. Students must log on every school day Monday through Friday to be counted for attendance.

Eligibility: Only students who are residents of the Riverside, San Bernardino, San Diego, Imperial, or Orange counties in California are eligible.

Online high school courses offered:

Algebra 1

Algebra 2

Art 1

Biology

Chemistry

Community Service

Composition

Consumer Math

Drama

Driver's Education

Earth Science

Economics

English 1

English 2

English 3

English 4

Geometry

Journalism

Life Science

Linguistics

Math Analysis

Physical Education

Physical Science

Poetry

Shakespeare

Spanish 1

Spanish 2

U.S. Government

U.S. History

Work Experience

World Geography

World History

Offers diploma? Yes

Tuition: As a public school, Choice 2000 is tuition free.

Computer requirements:

Pentium 4 or AMD processor

Microsoft Windows XP

512 MB RAM recommended (256 MB minimum)

20-GB hard drive

CD-ROM drive

Sound card

56-K modem (broadband Internet connection preferred)

Printer

Monitor (1024 x 768 resolution, 16-bit color)

Headset or microphone and speakers

Cable, DSL, or dial-up Internet access

Norton Antivirus (recommended)

Accreditation: Western Association of Schools and Colleges

Christa McAuliffe Academy

402 E. Yakima Avenue, Suite 1100
Yakima, WA 98901

Phone: Toll-free (866) 575-4989 or
(509) 575-4898

Fax: (509) 575-4976

Web site: http://www.cmacademy.org

E-mail: glen@cmacademy.org

Description: Christa McAuliffe
Academy is a K–12 private school
organized as a nonprofit 501(c) (3)
corporation. CMA emphasizes
individualized instruction using
computer courseware delivered over
the Internet. Student success is
measured by demonstrating
competence at 80% or better in each
subject at every level. Each student
determines his or her own pace and
learning style, but mastery of each
lesson is required to progress.

CMA contracts with certified teachers
who we refer to as mentors. They
provide academic assistance,
counseling, guidance, encouragement,
assessment, and caring support to
students. An important aspect of this
system is that students pick their own
mentor. As a result, close professional
relationships are formed, often
extending all the way through high
school graduation.

CMA has the distinction of being the
only accredited distance learning
school to have InterAct! for group
discussion and interaction with peers.
InterAct! is an advanced technology
system that we use to conduct
scheduled weekly online classes for all
full-time students. InterAct! provides
ample opportunity for the students to
learn and exchange ideas, to practice
communication skills, and to get to
know each other and their mentor in
real time. It also provides
opportunities for each student to
prepare and present lessons or
projects.

Eligibility: Anyone may apply.

Online high school courses offered:

A.P. U.S. History

Algebra I

Algebra II/Trigonometry

American History

American Literature

British Literature

Calculus

Chemistry

Civics

College Reading

Computer Skills

Drama

Earth Science

Earth/Space Science

Economics

French

Geometry

German

Honors World History

Korean

Occupational Education

Physical Education

Physical Science

Physics

continued on next page

Christa McAuliffe Academy
continued from previous page

Poetry and Short Stories

Process Writing

Senior Portfolio

Spanish

State History

Technical Writing

U.S. Government

World History

World Literature

Offers diploma? Yes

Tuition: $3,600 each year, or $325 for a half-credit course

Computer requirements:

266 MHz or faster computer

32 MB RAM

100 MB free disk space

Reliable Internet connection

Accreditation: Commission on International and Trans-Regional Accreditation

Northwest Association of Accredited Schools

Clark County School District Virtual High School

2501 Vegas Drive
Las Vegas, NV 89106

Phone: (702) 855-8435

Fax: (702) 855-8438

Web site: http://www.ccsdde.net

E-mail: distanceed@interact.ccsd.net

Description: The Virtual High School is the only public online high school in the Clark County School District.

The high school has evolved from the former Distance Education program. The high school began accepting full-time and part-time students in the fall 2004 school year.

Virtual High School is a distance education provider for the Clark County School District that promotes educational options through interactive online courses, televised instruction, and digital media for students in the state of Nevada. Since its inception in 1996, Virtual High School has enrolled thousands of students from comprehensive high schools and charter schools in video, television, and online courses.

Additional courses are offered each year in response to the needs of students in Clark County and other Nevada counties. Credits earned through the Virtual High School are recorded on students' high school transcripts upon completion of course work. Courses follow a traditional school year.

Eligibility: All residents of Clark County School District. In addition, students who are Nevada residents may enroll if their school board has signed an agreement with the Clark County School District.

Online high school courses offered:

A.P. Biology

A.P. Calculus BC

A.P. Chemistry

A.P. English Language and Composition

A.P. European History

A.P. French

A.P. Macroeconomics

A.P. Microeconomics

A.P. Physics B

A.P. Physics C

A.P. Psychology

A.P. Spanish

A.P. Statistics

A.P. U.S. Government

A.P. U.S. History

A.P. World History

Algebra I

Algebra I Honors

Algebra II

Applied Communications

Biology I

Biology I Honors

Business Law

Career Education

Chemistry I

Civil Liberties

College Survival

Computer Applications

Computer Science I

Consumer Education

Contemporary Math I

Contemporary Problems

Crime and Justice

Driver Education

English I

English I Honors

English I Read/Write

English II

English III

Environmental Science

French I

French II Honors

French III Honors

Geometry

Geopolitical Economics

Health

Math Applications

Modern Literature

Multicultural Themes in Literature

Personal Wellness I

Personal Wellness II

Physics I

Precalculus

Principles of Science

Psychology I

Reading for Proficiency

Spanish I

Spanish II Honors

Study Skills

Trigonometry

U.S. Government

U.S. Government Honors

U.S. History

World History

Writing for Proficiency

Offers diploma? Yes

Tuition: $95 per half credit

Computer requirements:

Windows 98, NT 4.0 (with Service Pack 4), or XP

Pentium 100 MHz

64 MB RAM

16-bit sound card

800 x 600 resolution, 256 colors

Microphone and speakers, or headset

100 MB free hard drive space

continued on next page

**Clark County School District
Virtual High School**
continued from previous page

Netscape 4.5 or IE 5.0 (or later)
browser

High-speed Internet connection

Accreditation: In application process
for Northwest Association of Schools
and Colleges

Clintondale Virtual High School

20674 Hall Road
Clinton Township, MI 48038

Phone: Toll-free (800) 297-2119

Fax: (586) 790-2883

Web site:
http://www.clintondalevhs.org

E-mail: teachers@clintondalevhs.org

Description: Clintondale Virtual High
School is a partner with Clintondale
Community Schools, which is located
in Clinton Township, Michigan. CVHS
is committed to providing top-quality,
online courses to students. These
courses meet the same requirements as
specified by the Clintondale
Community Schools for their public
school students. Our mission is to
create and promote student success by
offering quality educational programs,
delivered by caring professionals, at a
time and place of the student's
choosing. Courses are self-paced, and
enrollment is continuous.

Eligibility: Anyone may enroll.

Online high school courses offered:

Algebra

Basic Art

Biology

Earth Science

Economics

English I

English II

English III

Environmental Science

General Math

Geometry

Government

Introduction to Calculus

Physical Science

Prealgebra

U.S. History

World Geography

World History

Offers diploma? Yes

Tuition: $325 per class

Computer requirements:

Windows 95

Pentium 90 MHz

16 MB RAM

20 MB available drive space

Internet connection at 28.8 K and an
Internet e-mail account

Monitor with support for 800 x 600
resolution and support 16-bit color

VCR

CD-ROM drive

Printer and access to a fax machine

Microsoft Internet Explorer 4.0 or
higher or Netscape 4.0 or higher

Microsoft Word 97

Colorado Online Learning

13300 W. 2nd Place, Room 125
Lakewood, CO 80228

Phone: Toll-free (877) 293-5673 or
(303) 339-4080

Fax: (303) 339-4084

Web site: http://www.col.k12.co.us

E-mail: mpena@col.k12.co.us

Description: Colorado Online
Learning provides high-quality,
standards-based, online learning
options for students, teachers,
administrators, and others involved in
education in Colorado. Students may
complete courses at school or home.
Program generally follows a traditional
school-year calendar, but students
may enroll at any time.

Eligibility: Anyone may enroll, but
Colorado Online Learning prefers
enrollment through the local school.

Online high school courses offered:

Accounting

A.P. Calculus

A.P. English Literature and
Composition

ACT/SAT Math Review

Algebra I

Algebra II

American Government/Civics

Anatomy and Physiology

Astronomy

Biology

C++ Programming

Career Exploration

College Physics

Colorado History

Computer Animation: The Power of
Flash!

Consumer Law

English I

English II

English III

French I

Fundamental Math

Fundamentals in Science

Future Issues: Biotechnology

Geology

Geometry

German I

German II

Greek

Health

Introduction to Composition

Introduction to Sociology: The Study
of Human Relationships

Java Programming

Latin I

Latin II

Latin III

Latin IV

Math Modules

Personal Psychology: Living in a
Complex World

Personal Psychology: The Road to Self-
Discovery

PoetSpeak: Reading, Writing, and
Living Poetry

Prealgebra

Precalculus

Readers/Writers Workshop

continued on next page

Colorado Online Learning
continued from previous page

Science in Literature (The Pen and the Petri Dish)

Shakespearean Theater: The Comedies

Shakespearean Theater: The Tragedies

Spanish I

Spanish II

Spanish III

Spanish IV

U.S. History

Web Page Development

World Geography

World History

Offers diploma? No

Tuition: In most cases, school districts pay course fees on behalf of students. Students not affiliated with a Colorado school district are charged $300 per course per semester.

Computer requirements:

Windows 98, 98 SE, ME, NT, 2000, or XP

64 MB RAM

28.8-K modem (56 K recommended)

Sound card and speakers

Browser: Internet Explorer or Netscape

Monitor: 800 x 600 resolution, 256 colors

Accreditation: Commission on International and Trans-Regional Accreditation

North Central Association of Colleges and Schools

Colorado State Academy

5255 Marshall Street, Suite 120
Arvada, CO 80003

Phone: (303) 996-9606

Fax: (303) 996-9607

Web site:
http://www.onlinehighschool.net

E-mail: marlin@onlinehighschool.net

Description: Colorado State Academy is a computer-based school. It is organized to assist other schools, homeschools, adult students, dropouts, expelled, and at-risk students. It is designed to provide a sound education for grades 3–12 and leads to the completion of a high school diploma. The procedures used to deliver the education program are tutoring and home study, which make use of modern technology. All students are assumed to be responsible for the direction of their life and for the completion of the task they have chosen.

Eligibility: Anyone may enroll.

Online high school courses offered:

Accounting

Adult Composition

Adult Grammar

Adult Reading Comprehension

Adult Science

Adult U.S. Constitution

Adult Vocabulary

American History 11

American Literature

Art

Basic Science 9

Bible Study 9

Bible Study 10

Bible Study 11

Bible Study 12

Biology 10

Business Math

Chemistry 11

Consumer Math

Economics 12

English Literature

Government/Geography 9

Health

History of U.S. Constitution

Language Arts 9

Language Arts 10

Language Arts 11

Language Arts 12

Math 9

Math 10

Math 11

Math 12

Physical Exercise

Physics 12

Practical Math

Prealgebra

Spanish I

Spanish II

Vocational Experience

World History 10

Offers diploma? Yes

Columbus Public Schools Virtual High School

Columbus Public Schools
High School Curriculum/Career
Education Department
Northeast Career Center
3871 Stelzer Road
Columbus, OH 43219

Phone: (614) 365-5728

Web site:
http://www.columbus.k12.oh.us

Description: The Columbus Virtual High School is an online, electronic, and community-based approach for students to earn high school credits needed for graduation. The program offers 24/7 flexibility so participants can work toward their diploma on their own time and at their own pace.

Eligibility: Anyone can enroll.

Offers diploma? Yes

Tuition: None to residents of the Columbus City School District

CompuHigh / Whitmore School

515 Wilson Avenue
Morgantown, WV 26501

Phone: Toll-free (866) 859-0777

Fax: Toll-free (866) 870-0684

Web site: http://www.compuhigh.com

E-mail: Marianne@compuhigh.com

Description: CompuHigh seeks to provide a supportive, challenging, and alternate learning environment. Students are encouraged to be in charge of their education, giving them

continued on next page

CompuHigh/Whitmore School
continued from previous page

the opportunity to develop creativity, independence, responsibility, time management, and critical thinking skills. We emphasize mastery in all academic courses allowing students to view themselves as capable of achieving their educational goals. Students can enroll at any time, and courses are self-paced.

Eligibility: Anyone can enroll.

Online high school courses offered:

Algebra 1

Algebra 2

American Government

American History

Anatomy and Physiology

Art History

Basic Grammar

Biology

Career Planning

Chemistry

Community Service

English 9

English 10

English 11

English 12

English Writing

Environmental Science

Fitness and Safety

Geometry

Health

Hebrew I

Independent Study

Introduction to Web Design

Native American Literature

Physical Education

Practical Math

Prealgebra

Spanish I

Spanish II

Speech

Stress Management

Think About It

World Geography

Offers diploma? Yes

Tuition: $885 or more per year, or $275 per course

Accreditation: Commission on International and Trans-Regional Accreditation

North Central Association of Colleges and Schools

Cumberland County Schools' Web Academy

115 E. Mountain Drive
Fayetteville, NC 28306

Phone: (910) 484-3391

Fax: (910) 484-7244

Web site:
http://www.ccswebacademy.net

E-mail: bpoole@ccswebacademy.net

Description: The CCS Web Academy offers over 85 high school courses during regular session, plus a summer school session. Students around the country have the opportunity to participate in distance learning at the high school level. Courses are Web-based. Classes start in September and January. Summer session is offered. Classes are not self-paced.

Eligibility: All eligible high school students.

Online high school courses offered:

A.P. Biology

A.P. Calculus

A.P. Chemistry

A.P. Environmental Science

A.P. European History

A.P. English Language and Composition

A.P. English Literature and Composition

A.P. Physics

A.P. U. S. History

Advanced Functions and Modeling

Algebra I

Algebra II

Anatomy and Physiology

Art Appreciation

ASSET Prep

Astronomy Honors

Bible as History

Biology I

Business and Financial Management I

Business and Financial Management II

Business Law

Chemistry I

Civics and Economics

Civics and Economics Honors

Computerized Accounting I

Computerized Accounting II

Computer Applications I

Computer Applications II

Computer Applications III: E-Commerce

Criminal Justice I

Digital Communication Systems

Drafting

English I

English I Honors

English II

English III

English III Honors

English IV

English IV Honors

Environmental/Earth Science

Fundamentals of Technology

Geometry

German I

German II

German III Honors

German IV Honors

Health and Physical Education

Health Team Relations

Interior Design and Housing

Introduction to Philosophy

Journalism 1

Latin I

Latin II

Latin III Honors

Latin IV Honors

Leadership Development

Library Science

Life Management

Marketing

Marketing Management

Medical Sciences I

Music Appreciation

Music Theory

Parenting and Child Development

continued on next page

**Cumberland County Schools'
Web Academy**
continued from previous page

Physical Science

Physics

Precalculus (Honors)

Psychology

SAT Prep

Small Business/Entrepreneurship

Sociology

Spanish I

Spanish II

Spanish III Honors

Spanish IV Honors

Success 101

Technical Math I

Technical Math II

U.S. History

World Geography

World History

World History Honors

Offers diploma? No

Tuition: $400 per course

Computer requirements:

Pentium-class machine @ 500 MHz or higher

Windows 98 SE, ME, XP or 2000

128 MB RAM

5-GB EIDE or higher hard drive

56-K modem or better connectivity (cable modem or DSL)

If you have a cable modem or DSL, it is recommended that you have a 3Com or DLink Network Card

Full duplex sound

CD-ROM

Microsoft Internet Explorer 5.5 (with Service Pack 2 or higher)

SVGA Monitor

Accreditation: Commission on International and Trans-Regional Accreditation

Southern Association of Colleges and Schools

Cyber Oregon Online COOLSchool

905 4th Avenue SE
Albany, OR 97321-3199

Phone: Toll-free (877) 838-6038

Fax: (541) 926-6047

Web site:
http://www.coolschool.k12.or.us

E-mail: admin@coolschool.k12.or.us

Description: Linn Benton Lincoln Education Service District seeks to provide schools with electronic educational alternatives. We provide support and training for districts to establish Web-based educational programs, develop Web-based resources, and access to electronic solutions. LBL/COOLSchool is a project of LBL ESD's Electronic Learning Department. We operate as an online school that employs a principal, secretary, registrar, and 25 teachers from across the state to create and teach online courses. The teachers are Oregon-licensed and highly qualified. All courses are accredited and designed to meet Oregon content standards.

Eligibility: Anyone may enroll.

Online high school courses offered:

A.P. Calculus

A.P. Chemistry

A.P. English Literature and Composition

Algebra 1.1

Algebra 1.2

Algebra 2.1

Algebra 2.2

American Government

American History 1.1

American History 1.2

American Sign Language (ASL) 1.1

American Sign Language (ASL) 1.2

American Sign Language (ASL) 2.1

American Sign Language (ASL) 2.2

Artline: A Journey through Western Art History

Chemistry 1.1

Chemistry 1.2

Child Development

Classic Literature of the Western World

Computer-Based Study Strategies

Cyber Study Skills

Drawing

English 3.1

English 3.2

English on the Web

ESOL

General Biology 1.1

General Biology 1.2

Geometry 1.1

Geometry 1.2

Introductory Astronomy 1.1: The Solar System

Journalism

Latin 1.1

Latin 1.2

Latin 2.1

Latin 2.2

Life Management Skills

Natural History of Oregon Country

Oregon Government

Oregon Writers

Personal Finance

Poetry, Short Stories, and a Novel

Prealgebra 1.1

Prealgebra 1.2

Precalculus 1.1

Precalculus 1.2

Psychology 1.1: The Road to Self-Discovery

Psychology 1.2: Living in a Complex World

Social Studies on the Web

Spanish 1.1

Spanish 1.2

Spanish 2.1

Spanish 2.2

Understanding Economics

World Geography 1.1

World Geography 1.2

World History 1.1

World History 1.2

Writing With Style

Offers diploma? No

Tuition: A one-semester course costs $295 for Oregon residents and $345 for nonresidents

Accreditation: Northwest Association of Schools and Colleges

Delta Cyber School

P.O. Box 1672
Delta Junction, AK 99737

Phone: Toll-free in Alaska (877) 895-1043 or (907) 895-1043

Fax: (907) 895-5198

Web site: http://www.dcs.k12.ak.us

E-mail: pam.krepel@dcsmail.com

Description: Delta Cyber School is an online public school open to all Alaskan students ages 5–19. It is free of charge to any Alaskan student not attending another public school. Tuition-based courses are also available for public school students. All course work is delivered online and taught by Alaskan teachers. Our elementary program requires considerable parental involvement, but all middle school and high school course work is delivered and graded by our teachers; parents are asked to serve as mentors to encourage their students to work but are not required to do any teaching or grading. Students have immediate access to their teachers through instant Web conferencing and/or phone from 8:30 a.m. to 3:45 p.m. Monday through Friday.

Eligibility: Must be an Alaska resident.

Online high school courses offered:

A.P. English
Alaska History
Algebra I
Algebra II
Anatomy/Physiology
Applied Math
Auroras
Biology I
Botany
Calculus
Chemistry
Computers and the Internet
Consumer Math
Creative Writing
Desktop Publishing
Earth Science
English I
English II
English III
English IV
Exploring the Arts
General Math
General Science
Geometry
German I
German II
Health
Keyboarding
NASA
Oceanography
Photoshop Graphics
Physical Education
Physical Science
Prealgebra
Precalculus
SAT/ACT Prep
Spanish I
Spanish II
U.S. Government
U.S. History
Web Page Publishing
Western Civilization

World Geography

Writing for HSGQE

Zoology

Offers diploma? Yes

Tuition: $600 for a full year, or $300 per semester. Tuition is charged only for those already enrolled in a public school.

Dennison Online Internet School

P.O. Box 29781
Los Angeles, CA 90029

Phone: (818) 371-2001

Web site:
http://www.dennisononline.com

E-mail:
principal@dennisononline.com

Description: This is not just another school with a Web site. This Web site *is* a school—a junior/senior high school for English literate students worldwide. It's for parents who want the benefits of private education but not the responsibilities of homeschooling, and it's for young, independent explorers!

Eligibility: Students must be at least 12 years of age or able to read at the seventh grade level. Enroll and start any time year round.

Online high school courses offered:

The core curriculum qualifies students for high school graduation. It integrates language and literature, humanities, science and mathematics, fine arts and technology, and recreation and health. The core curriculum is taken by all students in all grades.

The expanded curriculum prepares students for college admission. It consists of the core curriculum plus electives. Students select courses based on interest and future plans.

Offers diploma? Yes

Tuition: Tuition is $3,000 per semester (six months' access). Materials are not included.

Computer requirements: PC or Mac with DVD multimedia capability

Accreditation: Accreditation Commission for International Internet Education

Eagle Christian School

2526 Sunset Lane
Missoula, MT 59804

Phone: Toll-free (888) EAGLE4U ext. 225 or (406) 542-0632 ext. 225

Fax: (406) 549-5047

Web site:
http://www.eaglechristian.org

E-mail: principal@eaglechristian.org

Description: Eagle Christian is an Internet school that began offering courses online in 1996 with 12 students. Even from those early days, our goal has been to provide a quality Christian education to students by encouraging them to make Christ preeminent in their lives. We strive to provide a well-designed and challenging course of study as we discipline young men and women to follow Jesus. We believe the Bible is the final authority by which everything must be evaluated. We were founded on a total commitment

continued on next page

Eagle Christian School

continued from previous page

to an interdenominational program. We seek to build online relationships through the Internet between our staff and your children. Our staff wants to communicate their passion to teach students who have a desire to learn. Classes follow a traditional school year. Summer classes are available.

Eligibility: Anyone may enroll.

Online high school courses offered:

A.P. English

Accounting (Quick Books)

Advanced Math

Advanced Spanish

Advanced Writing for Publication

Algebra 1

Algebra 2

American Literature

Anatomy and Physiology

Apologetics

Arithmetic

Beginning HTML

Beginning Spanish

Beginning Writing for Publications

Biology

British Literature

Calligraphy

Chemistry

Communication

Consumer Math

Drawing

Environmental Science

Geometry

Government and Economics

Great Books

Homiletics

Life in Christ

Microsoft Office

Music Appreciation

Music Theory

New Testament Survey

Old Testament Survey

Pastels

Personal Trainer

Physical Education

Physical Science

Physics

U.S. History

Watercolors

Web Design Internship

World Studies

Writing Lab

Offers diploma? Yes

Tuition: Tuition for a full time student (4–6 classes) is $875 per semester. Tuition for a part-time student is $275 per class per semester. Financial aid may be available.

Accreditation: Montana Federation of Independent Schools

Education Program for Gifted Youth

Ventura Hall
Stanford University
Stanford, CA 94305-4115

Phone: Toll-free (800) 372-EPGY or (650) 329-9920

Fax: (650) 329-9924

Web site: http://www.epgy.stanford.edu

E-mail: epgy-info@epgy.stanford.edu

Description: The Education Program for Gifted Youth at Stanford University is a continuing project dedicated to developing and offering multimedia computer-based distance learning courses. Combining technical and instructional expertise, EPGY provides high-ability students of all ages with an individualized educational experience, optimized in both pace and content. Through EPGY, students have access to courses in a variety of subjects at levels ranging from kindergarten through advanced undergraduate. Currently over 3,000 students from 28 countries are enrolled in EPGY. Most English courses meet online weekly and have fixed start and ending dates. Other courses start on the first of the month and are self-paced.

Eligibility: Applicants must submit scores from the SAT or another nationally recognized standardized test. Students seeking to take Expository Writing must also submit a writing sample.

Online high school courses offered:

A.P. English Language and Composition

Advanced Expository Writing

Calculus A

Calculus B

Calculus C

Compound Data Types and Advanced Topics in C

Fundamentals of Music Theory

Grammar and Style of the Sentence

Honors Beginning Algebra

Honors Geometry

Honors Intermediate Algebra

Honors Precalculus

Intermediate Expository Writing

Introduction to C Programming

Introduction to Java

Introductory Physics

Physics C: Electricity and Magnetism

Physics C: Mechanics

Programming in C – Algorithms and Techniques

Topics in Creative Writing

Offers diploma? No

Tuition: Ranges from $290 to $525. Financial aid is available.

Computer requirements:

Recommended:

200-MHz Pentium or better PC with at least 32 MB RAM

40 MB–90 MB free hard drive space

32-bit sound card and CD-ROM drive

Speakers or headphones

Internet access and the ability to send and receive e-mail and attachments on a daily basis

Accreditation: Western Association of Schools and Colleges

Eldorado Academy

P.O. Box 190
Nederland, CO 80466

Phone: (303) 604-2822

Fax: (303) 258-3541

Web site:
http://www.eldoradoacademy.org

E-mail:
president@eldoradoacademy.org

Description: The mission of Eldorado Academy is teaching students to acquire and apply knowledge, encouraging them to think critically, and communicate clearly as they become responsible, contributing members of our academic community and society at large. As an independent, private school specializing in distance learning for grades K–12, we welcome students of all abilities, backgrounds, and academic needs. The program at Eldorado Academy integrates learning and technologies, including the personal computer, Internet, telecommunications, e-mail, and other tools to deliver the best in educational curriculum, personalized progression, and learning support to its students.

The school's goal is to develop independent learners who confidently learn and progress to new material with minimal intervention. Eldorado believes the rate at which different students learn varies according to the individual and the conditions surrounding and impacting their learning environment. The instructional strategies at the school are designed to optimize these conditions, offering each student the best opportunity for academic success. Certified teachers implement educational programs that are tailored to the specific needs of each individual student. Eldorado Academy students also attend a virtual classroom for one hour each week. Integrating topics are discussed online, providing the opportunity for participation, idea generation, and interchange among students as facilitated by our teachers.

Eligibility: Anyone may enroll.

Online high school courses offered:

Accounting

Algebra I

Algebra II

Architecture

Biology

Calculus

Character Analysis

Chemistry

Geometry

Diseases and Disorders

Drama

Earth Science

Economics

Elements of Poetry

Geography and Modern World History

Grammar and Writing Mechanics

Health

Literary Elements

Major Authors

Modern Fiction and Nonfiction

Music

Nonfiction Literature

Novels

Periods of English Literature

Physical and Emotional Health

Physical Education

Physical Science

Physics

Poetry

Political Science

Protecting Yourself From Drugs

Psychology

Research

Short Stories

Sociology

State History and Community Study

Trigonometry

U.S. Government

U.S. History

Visual Arts

Western Civilization

Offers diploma? Yes

Tuition: $225 per student per month.

Computer requirements:

Pentium 200 MHz or comparable processor

32 MB RAM

2-GB hard drive

56-K modem

Windows 95/98/2000/NT/XP or MAC OS

Java-enabled Web browser: Internet Explorer or Netscape

Adobe Reader

Internet Service Provider (ISP) access

Accreditation: Commission on International and Trans-Regional Accreditation North Central Association on Accreditation and School Improvement

Electronic Classroom of Tomorrow

3700 S. High Street, Suite 95
Columbus, OH 43207-4083

Phone: Toll-free (888) 326-8395 or (614) 492-8884

Fax: (614) 492-8894

Web site: http://www.ecotohio.org

E-mail: info@ecotoh.org

Description: The Electronic Classroom of Tomorrow, based in Columbus, Ohio, has provided students throughout the state with a quality, online public education since the 2000–2001 school year. Regionally-based teachers, supported by a team of advisers, are committed to high performance standards and innovative educational methods. A growing number of graduates have earned their high school diplomas, and many more will follow in their footsteps. As an online public school, ECOT provides its students with a flexible, tuition-free alternative to traditional public education. ECOT is a national leader in this growing trend.

Eligibility: Any school-aged student residing in Ohio at the beginning of the school year may enroll.

Offers diploma? Yes

Tuition: No

Computer requirements: ECOT provides up to one computer per student at the option of the parent or provides allowances to students using their own computer. ECOT also offers each household a stipend for connecting to ECOT's secure Web-based network, or intranet.

Electronic High School

250 E. 500 S.

P.O. Box 144200

Salt Lake City, UT 84114-4200

Phone: (801) 538-7736 or (801) 538-7972

Fax: (801) 538-7877

Web site: http://ehs.uen.org

E-mail: ehs@uen.org

Description: The Electronic High School has been in operation since 1994 and provides a wide variety of courses to students across the world. Additional courses are added each year as interest and funding permit. The Electronic High School courses have been developed by master teachers and are correlated to the Utah State Core standards and objectives. We offer a flexible, open-entry/open-exit curriculum that is competency based. With a few exceptions, students are able to enroll any day of the year and work at their own pace until the course is completed. We expect students to complete a course within 12 months, but extensions can be granted.

Eligibility: Anyone may enroll.

Online high school courses offered:

Adult Roles and Responsibilities

Advertising and Promotion

American Sign Language

Ancient World Civilizations

Art Foundations

Art History and Criticism

Biology

Business Communication

Business Law

Business Webpage Design

Calculus

Chemistry

Child Development

Computer Programming C++

Computer Programming I – Java

Computer Technology

Danish I

Digital Photography

Driver and Traffic Safety Education

Dutch I

Dutch II

Earth Systems

Economics

Elementary Algebra

English 9

English 10

English 11

English 12

English as a Second Language

Financial Literacy

Fitness for Life

Food and Nutrition

Food and Science

French I

French II

Geography for Life

Geometry

German I

German II

Health Education II

Hebrew I

Hindi I

Horse Management

Human Biology

Indonesian I

Interior Design

Intermediate Algebra

Italian I and II

Japanese 1

Japanese 2

Journalism

Korean I

Latin 1

Latin 2

Latin 3

Medical Anatomy and Physiology

Modern World Civilizations

Music Aesthetics

Navajo Government

Navajo I

Navajo II

Pashto I

Photography

Physics: Electricity and Magnetism

Physics: Matter and Atomic Theory

Physics: Momentum and Energy

Physics: Motion and Waves

Polish I

Portuguese I and II

Prealgebra

Precalculus

Pre-engineering Technology

Principles of Technology

Psychology

Russian I and II

Sociology

Spanish 1 and 2

Spanish 5

Sports and Entertainment Marketing

Swahili I

Swedish I

Thai I

Turkish I

U.S. Government and Citizenship

U.S. History II

Vietnamese I

Welsh I

World Geography

Offers diploma? In some circumstances

Tuition: Students from outside Utah pay $100 per semester per class.

Computer requirements: Computer with Internet access

Accreditation: Northwest Association of Accredited Schools

Elkhart Cyber School

P.O. Box 999

150 Wildcat Avenue

Elkhart, KS 67950

Phone: Toll-free (866) 697-1166 or (620) 697-1166

Fax: (620) 697-2607

Web site: http://www.onlineecs.org

E-mail: shurn@onlineECS.org

Description: Elkhart Cyber School is one of the first in the state of Kansas and across the nation to offer an innovative, online, educational opportunity for students in grades K–12. Students complete course work both online and offline and communicate with their teachers and fellow classmates via chat rooms,

continued on next page

Elkhart Cyber School
continued from previous page

discussion boards, and e-mail, all from the comfort of home.

The goal of ECS is to provide students with a solid education through an alternative delivery method. Time and place take on new meaning when students have the flexibility to complete assignments at any time of day and from any location. While our delivery method may be flexible, our curriculum is solidly aligned with the rigorous Kansas State standards and is facilitated by Kansas certified instructors. Students completing the program earn a Kansas diploma. High school enrollment deadlines are in September and January.

Eligibility: Anyone may enroll.

Online high school courses offered:

Advanced Biology

Algebra I

Algebra II

Anatomy and Physiology

Art

Biology

British Literature

Business Computer Applications

Chemistry

Consumer Math

English Composition I and II

Foundations of Living

French I

General Business

General Science

Geometry

Introduction to Journalism

Keyboarding

Language Arts 9

Language Arts 10

Language Arts 11

Music

Physical Education

Prealgebra

Psychology/Sociology

Skills Tutor

Spanish I

Spanish II

Speech

Street Law

U.S. Government

U.S. History

Web Design

World Geography

World History

Offers diploma? Yes

Tuition: Students who are Kansas residents are not charged tuition. Students from outside of Kansas are charged tuition. Single courses are available for $175 for a half-year course and $350 for a full-year course.

Accreditation: North Central Association of Colleges and Schools

E-School

Advanced Technology Research Office
475 22nd Avenue
Building 302, Room 211
Honolulu, HI 96816

Phone: (808) 733-4777

Fax: (808) 733-4730

Web site:
http://www.eschool.k12.hi.us

E-mail: atr@k12.hi.us

Description: E-School is a supplementary education program run by the Hawaii Department of Education out of the Advanced Technology Research Branch. It is designed to offer online distance education credit classes utilizing many digital technologies, including Internet communication tools such as Webpages, e-mail, threaded discussion, chat, streaming video, and online textbooks.

Eligibility: Limited to students in Hawaii.

Online high school courses offered:

A.P. Computer Science

Algebra IA "Algebra in a Virtual World"

Art Appreciation 1A

Design 1A

Design 2A: House and Interior Design

Directed Study in English Language Arts

Economics

English Language Arts I

English Language Arts II

English Language Arts III

English Language Arts IV

Entrepreneurship A

Ethnic Studies

Geometry A

Introduction to Computer: Advanced "Tools for the Information Age"

Japanese 1A

MathArt Connections: Math Applications IA

Modern History of Hawaii

Problem Solving – Math Magic

Reading Workshop

Spanish 1A

U.S. History and Government

World History and Culture

Offers diploma? No

Tuition: No fees for courses offered during the regular school year. For summer classes, tuition is $80 per half credit.

Evergreen Internet Academy

P.O. Box 8910
Vancouver, WA 98668-8910

Phone: (360) 604-4057

Fax: (360) 604-4115

Web site: http://eia.egreen.wednet.edu

E-mail: cyberschool@egreen.wednet.edu

Description:

The Evergreen Internet Academy serves students across Washington and beyond. We strive in every way to provide a quality education to a diverse student body.

Our courses are rigorously matched to the Washington State Essential Learnings, are accessible 24/7 from any site with Internet access, and are highly interactive, with teachers and a computer lab assistant available from 7 a.m. until 3 p.m. by phone, e-mail, or in person at our campus. Our courses are delivered entirely through the Internet, with student-teacher interactions by e-mail, by phone, and in person. Students study crafted lessons that may combine text, images,

continued on next page

Evergreen Internet Academy
continued from previous page

sound, and even video. Students work with their instructors to overcome difficulties and discuss topics with other students in course discussion boards.

Eligibility: Anyone of high school age may enroll.

Online high school courses offered:

A.P. Calculus AB

CWP: Economics

CWP: Modern Problems

Active Fitness

Algebra 1 – Integrated

Algebra 2 – Integrated

Algebra 3 – Integrated

Algebra 4 – Integrated American Literature 1

American Literature 2

Astronomy

Biology 1

Biology 2

Conceptual Physics

Creative Writing Digital Communication Tools

Family Health

Freshman English 1

Freshman English 2

Geology

Geometry 1 – Integrated

Geometry 2 – Integrated

Internet Explorations

Introduction to Web Page Design

Mythology

Pacific Northwest History

Physical Science 1

Physical Science 2

Precalculus/Trigonometry 1 and 2

Science Fiction/Fantasy

Sophomore English 1

Sophomore English 2

U.S. History 3

U.S. History 4

Weightlifting for Fitness

Offers diploma? Yes, through state and district

Tuition: Washington state residents may attend without cost. Others pay $300 per course.

Computer requirements:

Pentium 150-MHz processor (if PC); 040 processor (if Mac)

32 MB RAM

Windows 95 or higher

56.6-K modem

Printer

Accreditation: In process

Fairfax County Public Schools Online Campus

Sprague Technology Center
4414 Holborn Avenue
Annandale, VA 22003

Phone: (703) 503-7781

Fax: (703) 503-7786

Web site:
http://www.fcps.edu/DIS/onlinecampus/index.htm

E-mail: Sandy.Todd@fcps.edu

Description: FCPS Online Campus delivers courses identical in content to those offered in our traditional classrooms and use multimedia to engage students. These courses are aligned with the Virginia Standards of Learning and follow the Fairfax County Public Schools Program of Studies. Courses start in September and January. Summer courses also are offered.

Eligibility: Anyone may register.

Online high school courses offered:

A.P. Biology

A.P. Calculus AB

A.P. Chemistry

A.P. English Language and Composition

A.P. English Literature and Composition

A.P. French Language

A.P. French Literature

A.P. Macroeconomics

A.P. Microeconomics

A.P. Physics B

A.P. Psychology

A.P. Spanish Language

A.P. Statistics

A.P. U.S. Government and Politics

A.P. U.S. History

Algebra I

Algebra II

Biology I

Chemistry I

Creative Writing

English 9

English 10

English 11

English 12

Geometry

Geosystems

Physics I

Spanish I

Virginia and U.S. History

Virginia and U.S. Government

World History and Geography I

World History and Geography II

Offers diploma? No

Tuition: Fairfax County students are not charged. Others are charged $300 per semester course, or $600 per year-long course.

Computer requirements:

Pentium III 500-MHz Processor, with Windows 98 SE or later; or Macintosh computer with System 9.1 or later

128 MB RAM

Color monitor: 16-bit, 1024 x 768 recommended resolution, 800 x 600 minimum resolution

Keyboard and mouse

56-K modem

16-bit sound card and speakers

8x or faster CD-ROM drive

40-MB hard drive

Internet Service Provider (ISP)

Netscape 6.0 or higher or Internet Explorer 6.0 with plug-ins

Florida Virtual School

445 W. Amelia Street, Suite 301
Orlando, FL 32801

Phone: (407) 317-3326

Fax: (407) 317-7963

Web site: http://www.flvs.net

E-mail: info@flvs.net

Description: The mission of Florida Virtual School is to provide students with high-quality, technology-based educational opportunities to gain the knowledge and skills necessary to succeed in the 21st century. Courses are Web-based, and students can begin a course at any time.

Eligibility: Students in grades 6–12.

Online high school courses offered:

A.P. American History

A.P. Biology

A.P. Calculus AB

A.P. Computer Science A

A.P. Computer Science AB

A.P. English Language

A.P. English Literature

A.P. Art History

A.P. Macroeconomics

A.P. Microeconomics

A.P. U.S. Government

Algebra 1A

Algebra 1B

Algebra I/Algebra I Honors

Algebra II/Algebra II Honors

American Government/American Government Honors

American History/American History Honors

Biology/Biology Honors

Business Systems Technology

Chemistry/Chemistry Honors

Computer Programming Basic I

Earth Space Science/ESS Honors

Economics/Economics Honors

English I/English I Honors

English II/English II Honors

English III/English III Honors

English IV/English IV Honors

FCAT Prep – 10th Grade Review

Fitness Lifestyle Design

Geometry/Geometry Honors

Global Studies

Latin I

Latin II

Latin III

Liberal Arts Math

Life Management Skills

Marine Science/Marine Science Honors

Personal Fitness

Physics/Physics Honors

Precalculus

SAT Prep

Spanish I

Spanish II

Thinking and Learning Strategies

Web Design 1

Web Design 2

World History/World History Honors

Offers diploma? No

Tuition: No tuition for Florida residents. Nonresidents are charged $375 for a half-credit course ($400 for advanced placement), or $750 for a one-credit course ($800 for advanced placement).

Computer requirements:

PC Requirements:

Pentium II (233 MHz minimum, higher recommended)

128-K Internet connection. A broadband connection is recommended.

Windows 2000, 98, NT, XP, ME (Windows ME does not support software used in the following courses: Web Design 1 and 2)

256 MB RAM

12x CD-ROM (CD/DVD Recommended)

Display setting 1024 x 768 resolution

Printer

Internet Explorer 5.5 or higher

Flash 7 player

Students need a method to save work to a removable disk (floppy, Zip, CD-ROM)

Sound card with speakers, microphone, or headset (needed in some courses)

Macintosh Requirements:

Power Mac G3

OS X

Students need a method to save work to a removable disk (Floppy, Zip, CD-ROM)

128 MB RAM

12x CD-ROM (CD/DVD Recommended)

128-K Internet connection. A broadband connection is recommended.

Display setting 1024 x 768 resolution

Printer

Speakers and microphone or headset (needed in some courses)

Accreditation: Commission on International and Trans-Regional Education Southern Association of Colleges and Schools

The Francis School

4240 Amboy Road
Staten Island, NY 10308

Phone: (718) 967-0400

Fax: (718) 227-7766

Web site:
http://www.francisschool.com

E-mail: register@francisschool.com

Description: The Francis School is an accredited New York State high school that offers online courses for credit. All courses are developed by accomplished teachers in their subject areas. These lessons and activities are student driven and use the abundant wealth of information that is found on the Internet. By using the latest Internet technologies with content-specific courses, students are able to complete high school classes right from their own home.

Students may register at any time and work at their own pace. Teachers are available online through e-mail or via our real-time bulletin board system. Our help procedures allow students to be in contact with state-certified faculty members for assistance in any course. Along with academic support, The Francis School provides a

continued on next page

The Francis School
continued from previous page

technical support department to assist with any computer or Internet problems that may arise while taking a course.

Eligibility: Anyone may register. Students must be at least 18 years old to enroll in the diploma-granting program.

Online high school courses offered:

American Government

Biology

Chemistry

Economics

English 1

English 2

English 3

English 4

Environmental Science

Global History (First Year)

Global History (Second Year)

Mathematics A

Mathematics B

U.S. History

Offers diploma? Yes

Tuition: $275 to $350

Computer requirements:

An IBM-compatible computer running Windows 95 or higher equipped with a printer. Macintosh users may experience some minor inconveniences but can use The Francis Virtual School.

Word processing software (WordPad or Microsoft Word).

A Web browser (Microsoft Internet Explorer 5.0 or higher or Netscape Communicator 4.6 or higher). If you are using AOL or Prodigy, you may use their Web browser and e-mail system.

Additional software such as Shockwave, WinZip, Windows Media Player, and Real Player will assist you in viewing the Web sites more effectively and can be downloaded free. It is important you have a reliable Internet connection. You may use a dial-up or DSL connection. We suggest that your connection speed is 33.6 K or higher.

You must have an e-mail account that can send and receive attachments.

Accreditation: New York State Department of Education

Futures International High School

2204 El Camino Real, Suite 312
Oceanside, CA 92054

Phone: (760) 721-0121

Fax: (760) 721-6127

Web site:
http://www.internationalhigh.org

E-mail: info@futures.edu

Description: Students receive real-time, individualized instruction over the Internet using videoconferencing technology. Because instruction is individualized, assignments reflect the learning style and personal needs of each student. Students must master the assignment at 80% or better before moving on to the next assignment.

Eligibility: Anyone may enroll.

Online high school courses offered:

Advanced Music Theory

Algebra I

Algebra II

American Government

American Literature and Composition

Anatomy and Physiology

Anthropology

Art Appreciation

Astronomy and Space

Basic Math

Basic Music Theory

Biology

Business English

Calculus

Career Exploratory

Chemistry

Children's Literature

Computer Applications Basic

Computer Applications Advanced

Consumer Mathematics

Contemporary Living

Cultural Geography

Earth Science

Economics

English 9

English 10

English 11

English 12

French 1

French 2

Geometry

German 1

German 2

Health

Latin 1

Latin 2

Latin 3

Latin 4

Math Analysis

Music Appreciation

Physical Science

Physics

Precalculus

Psychology

Sociology

Spanish 1

Spanish 2

Spanish 3

Statistics

Theater Appreciation

U.S. History

U.S. Military History

World History

World Literature and Composition

Offers diploma? Yes

Tuition: $750 per semester course

Computer requirements:

Headset with microphone

HyperPen stylus with touchpad (for science and math classes)

Microsoft Windows 98, ME, 2000, or XP (Windows XP Service Pack 2 recommended)

Microsoft Office Professional 2000, XP, or 2003

Horizon Wimba

Internet Explorer 5.5 or better

Antivirus software with updated antivirus definitions

A broadband Internet connection (DSL or cable) is required.

Accreditation: Distance Education and Training Council

Garden Schools

Rural Route 6, Box 6147
Ava, MO 65608

Phone: (417) 683-2111

Fax: (417) 683-2111

Web site:
http://www.gardenschools.com

E-mail: enroll@gardenschools.com

Description: Garden Schools is Christian distance learning for K–12 with a focus on ages 12–18. The curriculum is not designed to support individual courses. All course work is integrated so that children are accomplishing many subjects at the same time. While students do learn traditional topics, it is not a traditional format. All instruction occurs online. Students receive their assignments and turn in their work through this Web site.

Eligibility: Anyone may register.

Offers diploma? Not at present

Tuition: $4,500 each year

Accreditation: Not at present; working toward accreditation by the Association of Christian Schools International

Georgia Virtual School

Georgia Department of Education
1970 Twin Towers E.
205 Jesse Hill Jr. Drive
Atlanta, GA 30334

Phone: (404) 656-2183

Web site:
http://www.gavirtualschool.org

E-mail: GAVirtualHS@doe.k12.ga.us

Description: The Georgia Virtual School, an education initiative of the Department of Education, provides opportunities and options for Georgia students to engage in advanced placement, college preparatory, career and technical, and other electives online to enhance their learning experiences. You can take classes during the regular school day for no cost under the state and local rules established to govern the program. In addition, supplemental classes may be taken during fall, spring, and summer semester for tuition.

Eligibility: Anyone may enroll.

Online high school courses offered:

A.P. Biology

A.P. Calculus AB

A.P. Comparative Government

A.P. English Language and Composition

A.P. Macroeconomics

A.P. Microeconomics

A.P. Physics B

A.P. Psychology

A.P. U.S. Government and Politics

A.P. World History

Advanced Algebra and Trigonometry

Advanced Composition

Algebra I

Algebra II

Algebra III

American Government

American Literature and Composition

Biology I

Chemistry I

Civics/Citizenship

Computer Applications I

Economics

English Literature and Composition

Euclidean Geometry

Health/P.E.

Introduction to HTML

Latin I

Latin II

Literature and Composition, 9th Grade

Literature and Composition, 10th Grade

Physical Science

Physics

Psychology

SAT Prep

Statistics

Test Preparation

U.S. History

Web Page Design

World Geography

World History

World Literature and Composition

Offers diploma? No

Tuition: Free to Georgia residents taking courses as part of their regular class schedule. Summer and supplemental courses cost $300 for a half-credit course and $600 for a full-credit course. Out-of-state residents pay an additional $50.

Computer requirements:

Windows-based computers:

Windows 95, 98, 98 SE, ME, NT, 2000, or XP

233-MHz Pentium processor

32 MB RAM (64 MB recommended)

Sound card and speakers

Macintosh computers:

Mac OS 8.1–9.1 (OS X 10.1 in "classic mode")

32 MB RAM (64 MB recommended)

Sound card and speakers

The Grace Academy

10 Shurs Lane
Philadelphia, PA 19127

Phone: Toll-free (866) FOR-GRACE

Web site:
http://www.thegraceacademy.org

E-mail:
postmaster@thegraceacademy.org

Description: The Grace Academy is a Christian curriculum provider and learning resource center! It integrates the best qualities of several education options—Christian learning, private tutoring, and homeschooling. It gives you powerful tools, wise expertise, and gentle assistance that will enable you to give your child a quality education. The Grace Academy teaching teams are available during regular school hours to help students and parents.

Eligibility: Anyone may enroll.

Online high school courses offered:

A.P. Biology

A.P. English Language

A.P. English Literature

A.P. European History

A.P. French Language

A.P. U.S. History

Bible 9: New Testament

continued on next page

The Grace Academy
continued from previous page

Bible 10: Old Testament

Bible 11: Authentic Christian Living

Bible 12: Solid Ground Theology

Christian Evangelism

Christian Fantasy and Fiction

Christian Manhood

Christian Womanhood

Cinema History

Creative Writing

Discovering God's Creation Science: Science 9–12: Biology

Discovering God's Creation Science: Science 10–12: Chemistry

Discovering God's Creation Science: Science 11–12: Physics

Driver's Education

English 9: Creative Composition

English 10: Writing With Wisdom

English 11: Exploration and Expression

English 12: Celebrating the Classics

French 1

French 2

German 1

Introduction to Business

Introduction to Law

Introduction to Psychology

Introduction to Sociology

Journalism

Latin 1

Life Skills

Math 7–12: Algebra 1

Math 7–12: Algebra 1 with Saxon

Math 8–12: Geometry

Math 8–12: Integrated 1

Math 9–12: Algebra 2

Math 9–12: Algebra 2 with Saxon

Math 9–12: Consumer Math

Math 10–12: Trigonometry

Math 11–12: Calculus

Media Arts

Music: 20th Century Music

Music: Art and Music 9–12: Continuing your Exploration

Music: Christian Symbolism in Fine Art

Music: History of Christian Music

Music: Music Studio

SAT, College and Career Preparation

Social Action

Social Studies 9–12: Government and Economics

Social Studies 10–12: World History

Social Studies 11–12: World Religions

Spanish 1

Spanish 2

Video Game Development

Video Studio

Web Design

Wonderfully Made Health and Physical Education: Health and Physical Education 9–12: Dealing With Dangers

Offers diploma? No

Tuition: $1,800 (early enrollment discounts available)

Computer requirements:

Pentium III Processor

64 KB RAM

6-GB hard drive

Floppy drive

CD-ROM drive

56-K modem

Windows 98 or higher

Printer is highly recommended

Accreditation: National Private Schools Accreditation Alliance

Gwinnett County Online Campus

P.O. Box 343
Lawrenceville, GA 30046-0343

Phone: (770) 326-8082

Web site:
http://www.gwinnettk12online.net

E-mail:
gwinnettonline@gwinnett.k12.ga.us

Description: Online learning offers quality academic instruction with the flexibility of completing courses outside the traditional classroom setting. Online students must be self-motivated, independent learners. Students may attend class at any time of the day. However, you are required to log in to class daily.

Eligibility: Anyone may register.

Online high school courses offered:

A.P. American Government and Politics

A.P. Calculus AB

A.P. English Literature and Composition

A.P. Macroeconomics

A.P. Psychology

A.P. Statistics

A.P. World History

College Preparatory Biology

College Preparatory Chemistry

College Preparatory Composition Workshop

College Preparatory Economics

College Preparatory Freshman Language Arts

College Preparatory Junior Language Arts

College Preparatory Physics

College Preparatory Political Systems

College Preparatory Senior Language Arts

College Preparatory Sophomore Language Arts

College Preparatory U.S. History, 1st Semester

College Preparatory World Geography

College Preparatory World History

Accelerated Algebra II/Trigonometry

Advanced Algebra & Trigonometry

Advanced Placement Computer Programming (JAVA)

Advanced Web Page Design

Algebra 1

Algebra 2

Business Law

Concepts of Algebra

Concepts of Problem Solving

Controversial Issues

Discrete Math

Ethics and the Law

First Responder

French 2

Geometry

continued on next page

Gwinnett County Online Campus
continued from previous page

German 2

Honors Economics

Informal Geometry

Introduction to Health

Introduction to Lifetime Fitness

Latin I

Latin II

Law

Mathematical Money Management

Multimedia

Psychology

SAT I Prep

Sociology

Spanish 2

Statistics

Technical Junior Language Arts

Technical Senior Language Arts

Technical Chemistry

Technical Economics

Technical Physics

Technical Political Systems

Technical Sophomore Language Arts

Technical U.S. History

Web Page Design

Offers diploma? No

Tuition: $300 per course. Students not currently enrolled in a Gwinnett County public school pay an additional $40.

Computer requirements:

Windows-based computers:

Windows ME, 2000, or XP

64 MB RAM

28.8-K modem (56 K recommended)

Sound card and speakers

At least one of the following browsers: Internet Explorer 6.0 (recommended); Internet Explorer 5.5; Netscape Communicator 7.1 (recommended); Netscape Communicator 6.2

Macintosh computers:

Mac OS 9.1 and OS X

32 MB RAM (64 MB recommended)

28.8-K modem (56 K recommended)

Sound card and speakers

At least one of the following browsers: Internet Explorer 5.1x, 5.2x (recommended); Netscape Communicator 7.1 (recommended); Safari 1.2

Accreditation: Southern Association of Colleges and Schools

Houston Independent School District Virtual School

5827 Chimney Rock Road, Suite 1009 Houston, TX 77081

Phone: Toll-free (800) 306-4548 or (713) 349-2062

Fax: (713) 349-2051

Web site:
http://vschool.houstonisd.org

E-mail: VSchool@houstonisd.org

Description: HISD Virtual School exists in cyberspace, virtually everywhere. This allows for two-way interactive learning anytime, anywhere, and for any student. This innovative electronic format of instructional delivery is bringing the future to many students. Through participation in the HISD Virtual School, students acquire the skills needed to succeed in an increasingly technological world. Online learning in the HISD Virtual School helps students master course content, as well as develop communication, collaboration, and creative problem-solving skills. Students' technological fluency increases as they become adept at using computers and the Internet as a part of their learning.

As corporations have started using the Web for staff professional development, the HISD Virtual School is using the Web to help students become independent lifelong learners, able to locate and process information from a variety of sources, and communicate that learning to others.

Eligibility: Anyone may enroll.

Online high school courses offered:

Algebra I

Algebra II

Biology

Business Computer Information Systems

Chemistry

Communication Applications

Economics with Emphasis on the Free Enterprise System and Its Benefits

English I

English II

English III

English IV

French I

French II

Geology

Geometry

German I

German II

Health I

Individual and Family Life

Integrated Physics and Chemistry

Mathematical Models with Applications

Physics

Precalculus

Spanish I

Spanish II

Spanish III

U.S. Government

U.S. History Studies Since Reconstruction

World Geography

World History Studies

Offers diploma? No

Tuition: In district $150. Out of district $200

Computer requirements:

Any computer running an Internet browser such as Internet Explorer 6.0 or above (best viewed with Internet Explorer)

80 MB available hard drive space

A sound card, speakers, SVGA video card

A CD-ROM drive and a printer

Reliable Internet access: minimum 56-K modem

Office Suite software compatible with Microsoft

Office 97 (must include word processing, spreadsheet, and presentation applications)

RealPlayer software

Adobe Acrobat Reader 5.0

Macromedia Flash Player 6.0

Illinois Virtual High School

Illinois Mathematics and Science
Academy
1500 W. Sullivan Road
Aurora, IL 60506

Phone: (303) 873-0005

Fax: (630) 907-5072

Web site: http://www.ivhs.org

E-mail: wicks@imsa.edu

Description: The Illinois Virtual High
School is an Internet educational
service delivering a wide range of
quality high school class content
online to Illinois students. IVHS is a
supplement and complement to your
regular high school program.

Eligibility: A student must be
registered at a participating public
high school in Illinois.

Online high school courses offered:

A.P. Exam Review

A.P. Biology

A.P. Calculus AB

A.P. Chemistry

A.P. English Language and
Composition

A.P. English Literature and
Composition

A.P. Environmental Science

A.P. European History

A.P. French

A.P. Human Geography

A.P. Macroeconomics

A.P. Microeconomics

A.P. Physics B

A.P. Physics C

A.P. Psychology

A.P. Spanish

A.P. Statistics

A.P. U.S. Government and Politics

A.P. U.S. History

ACT Exam Preparation

Algebra 1

Algebra 2

American Government: Inside
Washington

American History 1

American Literature

Anthropology

Art History: Earliest Beginnings to
Classical Art

Art History: From the Renaissance to
Twentieth Century Art

Assembly Language Programming

Astrophysics

Beginning Composition

Biology 1

Biotechnology

Business and Personal Protocol

Business Communications

Calculus and Analytical Geometry I

Calculus and Analytical Geometry II

Career Planning: Exploration and
Decision Making

CCNA (Cisco Certified Network
Associate) Preparation

Chemistry

Civics in Cyberspace

Consumer Education

Creative Writing

Ecology

English 1

English 2

French I

French II

Geology

Geometry

German I

German II

Health Science 1

Information Processing

International Business

Introduction to Theatre

Latin I

Latin II

Macroeconomics

Networking Basics

Oceanography

Personal and Interpersonal Development

Personal Economics and Finance

Physics 1

Precalculus 1A: Analytical Geometry and Algebra

Precalculus 1A: Trigonometry

Psychology

Spanish I

Spanish II

Spanish III

Spanish IV

Study Skills: Learning Fundamentals

Web Page Design

World Civilizations

World History

World Literature 1A

Offers diploma? No

Tuition: The student's school district is billed $195 for a one-semester course or $390 for a year-long course. The local school district decides whether to pay the fee itself or pass it on to the student.

Computer requirements:

Windows-based computers:

Windows ME, 2000, or XP

64 MB RAM

28.8-K modem (56 K recommended)

Sound card and speakers

At least one of the following browsers: Internet Explorer 6.0 (recommended); Internet Explorer 5.5; Netscape Communicator 7.1 (recommended); Netscape Communicator 6.2

Macintosh computers:

Mac OS 9.1 and OS X

32 MB RAM (64 MB recommended)

28.8-K modem (56 K recommended)

Sound card and speakers

At least one of the following browsers: Internet Explorer 5.1x, 5.2x (recommended), Netscape Communicator 7.1 (recommended), Safari 1.2 (supported)

Indiana University High School

Owen Hall

790 E. Kirkwood Avenue

Bloomington, IN 47405

Phone: Toll-free (800) 334-1011

Fax: (812) 855-2292

Web site:
http://scs.indiana.edu/hs/highschoolcourses.html

E-mail: scs@indiana.edu

continued on next page

Indiana University High School
continued from previous page

Description: The School of Continuing Studies offers more than 100 high school courses through its Independent Study Program. The courses are based on the approved curriculum for Indiana schools, substantially reflecting state Department of Education subject area standards. They require the equivalent amount of work and carry the same credit as similar courses offered in traditional high school classrooms. Courses are offered online and by correspondence. You may enroll at any time, and courses are self-paced. Course is to be completed within 12 months.

Eligibility: Anyone can enroll.

Online high school courses offered:

Advanced Composition

American Literature

Art History and Appreciation

Basic Composition

Biology Level I: First Semester

Business Mathematics: First Semester

Computer Literacy

Creative Writing: Fiction

Economics

English 9

English 10

English Literature

The Experience of Drama

German Level I

German Level II

Health Education: Basic Course

Literature of the Future

Mythology

Personal Finance

Physical Science: An Introduction to Chemistry

Physical Science: An Introduction to Physics

The Short Story

U.S. Government

U.S. History

Understanding and Improving Your Memory

Vocabulary for the College-Bound Student

Women Writers: Fiction and Autobiography

World History: First Semester

Offers diploma? Yes

Tuition: $60 for a half-credit course and $120 for a one-credit course

Accreditation: North Central Association of Colleges and Schools

Intelligent Education

2859 Paces Ferry Rd, Suite 1200, Overlook III

Atlanta, GA 30339

Phone: (770) 431-5100

Fax: (770) 431-5101

Web site: http://www.intelligented.com

E-mail: admin@intelligented.com

Description: We use technology to automate the non-value-added activities (correcting papers, grading tests and quizzes, and taking attendance), and repetitive tasks (writing lesson plans and developing lessons). In a traditional classroom model there is a limited amount of time available for one-on-one personal interaction. Intelligent Education's experienced staff uses a majority of their class time in personal contact with their students.

The courses (lessons, quizzes, and exercises) are available online. The online lessons frequently refer to the Internet, educational resources, manipulatives, and textbooks. Students work individually and/or collaboratively with other students and the teacher in their learning activities. Research shows that people learn best when they teach. In our learning centers, students are constantly engaged in teaching each other.

Eligibility: Anyone may enroll.

Online high school courses offered:

A.P. Art History

A.P. Biology

A.P. Calculus BC

A.P. Chemistry

A.P. Chemistry B

A.P. Computer Science A (JAVA)

A.P. Computer Science AB

A.P. English Literature and Composition

A.P. Environmental Science

A.P. European History

A.P. French Language

A.P. German Language

A.P. Government and Politics: Comparative

A.P. Government and Politics: United States

A.P. Human Geography

A.P. Latin Literature

A.P. Latin: Virgil

A.P. Macroeconomics

A.P. Microeconomics

A.P. Music Theory

A.P. Physics

A.P. Physics C (Electricity and Magnetism)

A.P. Physics C (Mechanics)

A.P. Psychology

A.P. Spanish Language

A.P. Spanish Literature

A.P. Statistics

A.P. U.S. History

A.P. World History

African American Literature (Honors)

Algebra 1

Algebra 2

American Civics

American Government (1 semester)

American History (Civil War and Reconstruction)

American History A (Beginnings to 1861)

American History B – (Reconstruction to Present)

American Literature

Animal Health

Astronomy (Honors)

Auto Repair

Automotives

Basic Accounting 1

Basic Accounting 2

Basic Cookery

Basic Math for Electronics

continued on next page

Intelligent Education
continued from previous page

Basic Pharmacology

Beginning Piano

Biology

British Literature

Business Management

C++

Calculus A (Honors/A.P.)

Calculus B (Honors/A.P.)

Chemistry

Children's Literature

Communications Skills

Computer Applications

Computer Science

Computerized Drawing

Computers for Farmers

Corrections in the 21st Century

Criminal Evidence

Criminal Investigation

Criminal Justice

Crop Science

Cultural Anthropology (Honors)

Database Management

Desktop Publishing

Economics

Electronics

Engineering Essentials

Engineering Fundamentals

English 9

English 10

Entrepreneurship and Small Business Management

Environmental Science

Essentials of Electronics

Floriculture: Introduction

French 1 A (Digital Text and CD Audio Program)

French 1 B

French 2

French 3

Fundamentals of Engineering Drawing

General Health

Genetics

Geology (Honors)

Geometry

German 1

German 2

German 3

History of Asia (Honors)

History of Egypt and Canaan

History of Medieval Britain

History of Religion

History of the Crusades

History of the Holocaust

Home Economics

HTML (Web Page Design): Introduction

Human Anatomy and Physiology

Human Growth and Development

International Business

Introduction to Animal Biology

Introduction to Criminal Justice

Introduction to Fiction

Introduction to the Internet

Introduction to Paralegal Studies

Introduction to Photography

Introduction to Business

Introduction to Business and Personal Law

Introduction to Design (Honors)

Introduction to Drawing

Introduction to Electrodynamics

Introduction to Engineering Drawing

Introduction to Environmental Engineering

Introduction to HTML (Web Page Design)

Introduction to Personal and Business Law

Introduction to Philosophy

Japanese 1

Japanese 2

Latin 1

Latin 2

Legal Research/Writing

Legal Studies

Marketing Essentials

Mechanical Drawing

Medical and Legal Ethics

Medical Assisting 1 (Honors)

Medical Studies

Medical Terminology

Meteorology

Mexican American Literature (Honors)

Modern Earth Science

Motorcycle Repair

Music Appreciation (Survey of Western Music)

Native American History (Honors)

Native American Literature (Honors)

Oceanography (Honors)

Office Management

Outlaws and Lawmen

Paramedic Essentials

Parenting

Personal Fitness (Self Study PE)

Physical Science

Physics

Pirates Throughout History

Practical Math

Prealgebra

Precalculus

Psychology

Resources of the Earth (Honors)

Russian 1

Russian 2

Science Fiction Film

Science Fiction Literature

Sign Language

Sociology

Spanish 1

Spanish 2

Spanish 3

Spreadsheets

Technology of Machine Tools

The Child Care Professional

Theatre Arts

Trigonometry

Trigonometry A (Honors)

Western Civilization (Honors)

Word Processing 1

Word Processing 2

World Geography

World History

World Literature

World Literature (Honors)

World Mythology

Offers diploma? Yes

Tuition: $250 to $500 per course

continued on next page

Intelligent Education
continued from previous page

Computer requirements:

IBM-compatible PCs should have at least a 486 processor; at least a 14.4-K modem for accessing the Internet; color monitor with graphics capability; Windows 95 or higher; and at least 16 MB RAM.

Macintosh computers should have 6.0 or higher operating system; at least a 14.4-K modem for accessing the Internet; color monitor with graphics capability; and at least 16 MB RAM.

Phone connection

E-mail address

Printer

Accreditation: Accrediting Commission for Independent Study

Internet Academy

32020 1st Avenue S., No. 109
Federal Way, WA 98003-5743

Phone: (253) 945-2230

Fax: (253) 945-2233

Web site: http://www.iacademy.org

E-mail: registrar@iacademy.org

Description: Internet Academy provides courses and teachers to students via the Internet. Washington State-certified teachers provide instruction to students in grades K–12. The program allows for innovative uses of technology, customized learning environments, and access to skilled instructors. Students take courses in order to complete requirements for graduation, to access courses that may not be available at their resident school, to pursue special interests and talents while remaining on schedule for graduation, and to continue to participate in a homeschool environment. Semesters start in September and January, with a summer term.

Eligibility: Anyone may enroll.

Online high school courses offered:

Algebra 1

Algebra 2

Algebra 3

Algebra 4

Beginning Algebra

Biology

Business Law

Career in Motion

Civics

Computer Applications

Creative Writing

Drawing

Earth Science 1

English (Freshman)

English (Sophomore)

Geometry

Health Choices

Honors Sophomore English

HS Keyboarding

Junior English

Pacific NW History

Personal Finance

Photography

Physical Science

Psychology

Reading for Life

Shakespeare

Success

Themes Lit. and Film

U.S. History

Visual Com

Web Design

World History

World Literature

Offers diploma? No

Tuition: Washington State public school students attend free if they are taking five or fewer classes between online and in-person combined. Washington State private school students may also qualify for free tuition. Other students pay $395 per semester-length course.

Computer requirements:

Windows-based computers:

Pentium 3 or comparable (Celeron, AMD, etc.)

Microsoft Windows 98 SE or better

16x CD-ROM

Broadband is preferred or 56-K modem

150 MB free space on your hard disk

128 MB RAM

Microsoft Internet Explorer (5.5 or higher) or Netscape 6.1 higher

Power Mac computers:

64 MB RAM

500-MB hard drive

16x CD-ROM

Broadband or 56-K modem

Netscape or Internet Explorer (5.0 or better)

Mac OS 9.0 or higher

Accreditation: Northwest Association of Accredited Schools

Internet High School

Richard Milburn High School
3421 Commission Court, Suite 201
Woodbridge, VA 22191

Phone: Toll-free (877) 888-WISE

Fax: (703) 494-6093

Web site: http://www.rmhs.org

E-mail: wise@rmhs.org

Description: Through RMHS, a secondary education pioneer, WISE offers online high school classes and instruction serving young people worldwide. Using a curriculum specifically designed for independent study and growth, WISE capitalizes on the way students learn best and utilizes the worldwide resources available on the Internet.

The WISE classroom is as large as the world and serves students at any geographic location. Stressing academic excellence and using the latest education technology, WISE delivers an education and diploma that helps students function in today's changing world. Each year, thousands of students interested in new learning environments opt for alternative approaches for a high school diploma. Using the world as a classroom, WISE is able to offer the best alternative available for high school completion.

Eligibility: Anyone may register.

Online high school courses offered:

Algebra I

Algebra II

Biology I

Chemistry I

continued on next page

Internet High School
continued from previous page

Consumer Math

Creative Writing

English 9

English 10

English 11

English 12

Environmental Science

Geometry

Introduction to Psychology

Introduction to Technology

U.S. Government

U.S. History

World History

Offers diploma? Yes

Tuition: $375

Computer requirements:

Windows-based computers:

Intel Pentium or 486 processor running one of the following Microsoft Windows operating systems: Microsoft Windows NT version 3.51 or 4.0; Microsoft Windows 95; Microsoft Windows for Workgroups version 3.11 and DOS version 3.31 or later; Microsoft Windows version 3.1 and DOS version 3.31 or later

Memory: 6 MB RAM (8 MB recommended) for Windows 3.1 and Windows for Workgroups 3.11; 8 MB RAM (16 MB recommended) for Windows 95 and Windows NT 3.51 or 4.0

Hard drive with 80 MB free space recommended; 60 MB free space minimum

Macintosh computers:

A Power Macintosh will perform best, but a Macintosh II-based Performa, Macintosh Quadra, PowerBook model, or any Macintosh supporting a 68030 or 68040 processor is fine. Note: Computers that can't run Notes include PowerBook 100s, SEs, and Classic Macs, and it's excruciating slow on an LC II. (Power Macintoshes)

Macintosh System software 7.5 or later

Memory: 24 MB RAM (40 MB recommended)

Hard drive with 50 MB free space (70 MB is recommended)

Macintosh-compatible display adapter and color monitor

An Apple-compatible printer (optional, but highly recommended)

Apple Shared Library Manager (required for all Macs)

Accreditation: Distance Education and Training Council

Internet Home School

3060 Hozoni Road
Prescott, AZ 86305

Phone: (928) 708-9404

Fax: (928) 708-9384

Web site:
http://www.Internethomeschool.com

E-mail:
julia@Internethomeschool.com

Description: Internet Home School is a fully accredited K–12 online school. Our unique program offers math, English, science, social science, health, computer science, foreign languages, and art history. Internet Home School provides online teachers for student instruction. Student records are available to parents through our specially designed grade book program.

Our mission is to provide excellent education through online resources. We dedicate ourselves to finding and developing creative ways to use technology for teaching and learning in an online home-based environment. Our school offers families an alternative to the traditional public education system.

Eligibility: Anyone may register.

Online high school courses offered:

Algebra 1/2

Algebra 1

Language Arts 9th Grade

Language Arts 10th Grade

Language Arts 11th Grade

Language Arts 12th Grade

Offers diploma? Yes

Tuition: $2,580 annually if the parent grades student work; $3,780 otherwise

Computer requirements:

300 MHz processor

500 MB hard drive space

64 MB of RAM memory

56-K modem

Full-duplex sound card

Microphone and speakers

Windows 98 operating system

Internet Explorer 5.01

Accreditation: Commission on International and Trans-Regional Accreditation

North Central Association of Colleges and Schools

iQ Academies

School District of Waukesha
222 Maple Avenue
Waukesha, WI 53186

Phone: Toll-free (866) GOTO-iQA (866-468-6472)

Web site: http://www.go2iq.com

E-mail: info@iQacademies.com

Description:

iQ Academies launched in spring 2004 under a charter issued by the Waukesha Public School District in Waukesha, Wisconsin, and in partnership with KC Distance Learning Inc. Once enrolled, students receive a laptop computer, a quarterly stipend to cover the cost of Internet service, and textbooks required for their courses. As in traditional public schools, these learning tools are provided to our students at no cost for as long as they are enrolled in iQ Academies in Wisconsin. Some school administrative and student fees may apply.

Eligibility: iQ is tuition free for Wisconsin residents who enroll during the open enrollment period early in the year.

Online high school courses offered:

A.P. Art History

A.P. Biology

A.P. Calculus AB

A.P. Calculus BC

A.P. Chemistry

A.P. English

A.P. French

A.P. Physics

continued on next page

iQ Academies
continued from previous page

A.P. Spanish

A.P. U.S. History

Algebra 1 and 2

Algebra 2 (Honors)

American Government

American Government (Honors)

American Literature A and B

Beginning Composition

Biology

Chemistry

Composition: Advanced

Computer Applications 1

Earth Science

Economics

English 9

English 10

English 11

English 12

English 9 (Honors)

English 10 (Honors)

English 11 (Honors)

Fine Arts Independent Study Option

French 1 and 2

Geography

Geometry

Geometry (Honors)

German 1 and 2

Global Business Communication

Graphic Design A and B

Health and Physical Fitness

Keyboarding and Word Processing

Music Appreciation

Personal Economics and Finance

Physical Fitness Independent Study Option

Physics

Prealgebra

Precalculus and Trigonometry

Precalculus and Trigonometry (Honors)

Psychology

Reading Comprehension

Spanish 1 and 2

U.S. History

Web Design A (HTML)

Web Design B (JavaScript)

World Civilizations A and B

World History

Offers diploma? Yes

Tuition: iQ is tuition free for Wisconsin residents who enroll during the open enrollment period early in the year.

James Madison High School Online

P.O. Box 922697
Norcross, GA 30010-2697

Phone: Toll-free (800) 691-2901

Fax: (770) 729-8400

Web site: http://www.jmhsonline.com

E-mail: info@jmhsonline.com

Description: James Madison High School Online offers an exciting, flexible way to obtain an academically rigorous 9th through 12th grade education. Students of all ages and backgrounds have the freedom to complete our regionally and nationally accredited, Web-driven, 24-course curriculum anytime, any place. Our school is an excellent choice for students who travel or who need to make up failed courses, homeschoolers, and anyone who requires a nationally accredited diploma.

Eligibility: Anyone may enroll.

Online high school courses offered:

Algebra I

Algebra II

American Government

American History

American Literature

Art History

Biology

Biology Lab

British Literature

Business Systems Technology

Chemistry Lab

Economics

Emergent Computer Technology

Geometry

Health

Marine Science

Online Journalism

Physical Science Lab

Physics

Physics Lab

Precalculus

Psychology

Spanish I

Spanish II

Survey of Literature

World History

World Literature

Offers diploma? Yes

Tuition: $199 to $350 per course

Computer requirements:

Windows-based computers:

Windows 98 or higher

Microsoft Office 2000, XP, or 2003

128 MB RAM

20-GB hard drive or larger

56.6-K modem or DSL or cable modem

Super VGA (800 x 600 or higher resolution) video adapter and monitor

Sound card with speakers

CD-ROM (CD-RW recommended for saving large files)

Internet service provider (ISP) account

A current antivirus application (Norton Antivirus preferred)

Microsoft Internet Explorer Version 5.0 or later

Java 2 Runtime Environment

Flash Player 6

Adobe Acrobat Reader

Macintosh computers:

OS X operating system

Netscape Navigator 6.0 or Mozilla Firefox 1.6

Java – JRE v1.4.2.xx

Accreditation: Commission on International and Trans-Regional Accreditation

Distance Education and Training Council

Southern Association of Colleges and Schools

JeffcoNet Academy

McLain Community High School
13600 W. 2nd Place
Lakewood, CO 80228

Phone: (303) 982-8659

Web site:
http://online.jeffco.k12.co.us/login/jnet_index.htm

E-mail: secretary@jeffconet.org

Description: JeffcoNet Academy is the Jefferson County School District's online education provider. Our students take a full-time schedule of five or six courses online rather than attending a traditional high school program. We offer a full academic schedule, including courses in all of the core subject areas as well as electives. Online education provides a home-based educational environment, with support from licensed staff, using standards-based curriculum. JeffcoNet Academy provides a unique pathway to a high school diploma.

Offers diploma? Yes

Tuition: Free

The Jubilee Academy

446 N. Wells, Box 331
Chicago, IL 60610

Phone: Toll-free (866) JUB-ACAD

Web site:
http://www.thejubileeacademy.org

E-mail:
postmaster@thejubileeacademy.org

Description: The Jubilee Academy is a nationally recognized Christian curriculum provider for K–12 homeschoolers. The Jubilee Academy provides everything your child needs to receive an outstanding education at home. anytime, any place. Instruction follows a standard school year, with 300 days of instruction.

Eligibility: Anyone may enroll.

Online high school courses offered:

A.P. Biology

A.P. English Language

A.P. English Literature

A.P. European History

A.P. French Language

A.P. U.S. History

20th Century Music

Algebra 1

Algebra 1 with Saxon

Algebra 2

Algebra 2 with Saxon

Art and Music 9–12: Continuing Your Exploration

Bible 9: New Testament

Bible 10: Old Testament

Bible 11: Authentic Christian Living

Bible 12: Solid Ground Theology

Calculus

Christian Evangelism

Christian Manhood

Christian Symbolism in Fine Art

Christian Womanhood

Cinema History

Consumer Math

Discovering God's Creation Science: Science 9–12: Biology

Discovering God's Creation Science: Science 10–12: Chemistry

Discovering God's Creation Science: Science 11–12: Physics

Driver's Education

French 1

French 2

Geometry

German 1

Health and Physical Education 9–12: Dealing With Dangers

History of Christian Music

Introduction to Business

Introduction to Law

Introduction to Psychology

Introduction to Sociology

Christian Fantasy and Fiction

Creative Writing

English 9: Creative Composition

English 10: Writing with Wisdom

English 11: Exploration and Expression

English 12: Celebrating the Classics

Journalism

Latin 1

Life Skills

Math 8–12: Integrated 1

Media Arts

Music Studio

SAT, College and Career Preparation

Social Action

Social Studies 9–12: Government and Economics

Social Studies 10–12: World History

Social Studies 11–12: World Religions

Spanish 1

Spanish 2

Trigonometry

Video Game Development

Video Studio

Web Design

Offers diploma? No

Tuition: $799.95 for a year (early enrollment discounts available)

Computer requirements: Pentium III processor, 64 MB RAM, 6-GB hard drive, floppy drive, CD-ROM drive, and a 56-K modem or faster connection. We highly suggest a printer.

Accreditation: National Private Schools Accreditation Alliance

K–12 Distance Learning Academy

Oklahoma State University
K–12 Distance Learning Academy
213 LSE
Stillwater, OK 74078

Phone: Toll-free (800) 452-2787 or (405) 744-5647

Fax: (405) 744-6992

Web site: http://k12.okstate.edu

E-mail: cas-ext@okstate.edu

Description: The K–12 Distance Learning Academy from Oklahoma State University provides instruction and support for students, teachers, and administrators of grades 3–12.

Eligibility: Anyone may enroll.

Online high school courses offered:

A.P. Calculus AB

A.P. Calculus BC

A.P. German

Calculus I

Composition II

Computer Literacy

German I

continued on next page

K–12 Distance Learning Academy
continued from previous page

German II

German III

German IV

Introduction to Creative Writing

Introduction to Cultural Geography

Introduction to Music

Spanish I

Spanish II

Offers diploma? No

Tuition: Ranges from $389 to $830.

Computer requirements:

For German/Spanish classes: a fairly fast computer and high-speed Internet connection are needed. A minimum would be a Pentium II, 450 MHz, or a Mac G3 computer with a 56-K modem. A T1, DSL, or cable modem connection is best for accessing video clips and sound files.

Video clips and sound files require RealPlayer.

Animation clips require Flash Animation player.

Web browsers Internet Explorer 6.x or Netscape 7.x are recommended.

A high-quality speakerphone is required in the classroom for weekly phone sessions.

Karval Online Education

316232 County Road 29
P.O. Box 5
Karval, CO 80823

Phone: Toll-free (866) 375-3404

Fax: (719) 446-5331

Web site: http://www.ko-le.com

E-mail: sbook@karvalonlineeducation.com

Description: Karval OnLine Education (KOLE) is a public school fully online program accredited by the state of Colorado. KOLE is a member of the Colorado Cyberschool Association. We provide a well-designed and enriched course of study to students in grades K–12 throughout the state of Colorado. Our teachers have a clear passion for education and learning, and all are Colorado certified. Our curriculum is aligned with Colorado State standards, and we offer dual credit courses for juniors and seniors desiring college courses while meeting our high school graduation requirements. KOLE provides a dynamic education with the flexibility to meet individual student needs at their desired place and time, at no cost to the student or family.

Eligibility: Students must be Colorado residents and must have previously been enrolled in a Colorado public school.

Online high school courses offered:

Algebra I

Algebra II

American History I

American History II

Anthropology

Biology

Business and Consumer Math:

Business and Personal Protocol

Business Communication

Calculus I

Calculus II

Career Planning

Chemistry I

Chemistry II

Earth and Space

Economics

English 1

English 2

English 3

English 4

Geometry

Government

Health

History of the World I

History of the World II

Introduction to Psychology

Introduction to Technology

Life Science – Oceanography

Macroeconomics

Math Skills Review

Personal Economics and Finance

Physics

Prealgebra

Reading Comprehension

Real World Math

Spanish 1

Spanish 2

Study Skills

Trigonometry

World Geography

Offers diploma? Yes

Tuition: None

Computer requirements: The student will be provided with an appropriate computer.

Accreditation: State of Colorado

Kentucky Virtual High School

19th Floor, Capital Plaza Tower
500 Mero Street
Frankfort, KY 40601

Phone: Toll-free (866) 432-0008 or (502) 564-4772

Fax: (502) 564-6470

Web site: http://www.kvhs.org

Description: The Kentucky Virtual High School is an educational service managed by the Kentucky Department of Education to expand student access to challenging high school curriculum. Through the KVHS, Kentucky students have access to a wider range of course work, more flexibility in scheduling, the opportunity to develop capacities as independent learners, and increased time and opportunity to achieve, because learning online is neither time nor place dependent. KVHS courses are open 24 hours a day, seven days a week.

Eligibility: Open to students approved by their local school district.

Online high school courses offered:

A.P. Art History

A.P. Biology

A.P. Calculus AB

A.P. Calculus BC

A.P. Chemistry

A.P. Computer Science

A.P. English Language and Composition

A.P. English Literature and Composition

A.P. Environmental Science

continued on next page

Kentucky Virtual High School
continued from previous page

A.P. European History
A.P. French Language
A.P. German Language
A.P. Macroeconomics
A.P. Microeconomics
A.P. Physics B
A.P. Psychology
A.P. Spanish Language
A.P. Statistics
A.P. U.S. Government and Politics
A.P. U.S. History
Algebra I
Algebra II
American History
Biology
Chemistry
Earth and Space Science
English I
English II
English III
English IV
French I
French II
French III
Geometry
German I
German II
German III
Latin I
Latin II
Latin III
Latin Literature/A.P. Optional
Living, Learning and Earning:
Consumer Economics
Physics
Physics (Honors)
Physics II
Prealgebra
Precalculus
Spanish I
Spanish II
Spanish III

Offers diploma? No

Tuition: $220 for a half-credit course or one-semester A.P. course, or $400 for a full-credit or a two-semester A.P. course

Computer requirements:

Windows-based computers:

For ClassLive (synchronous tool): 64 MB RAM and Sun's Java 2 JRE (Java 1.3.1)

For ClassLive Audio: 56-K or higher modem and Windows Media Player 9

Macintosh computers:

For ClassLive (synchronous tool): 128 MB RAM; Microsoft Internet Explorer 5.1, 5.2 or higher (Macintosh OS); Mac OS Classic Java (MRJ 2.2.5)

For ClassLive Audio: Windows Media Player 7.1

Keystone National High School

420 W. 5th Street
Bloomsburg, PA 17815-1564

Phone: Toll-free (800) 255-4937 or
(570) 784-5220

Fax: (570) 784-2129

Web site:
http://www.keystonehighschool.com

E-mail: info@keystonehighschool.com

Description: For over 30 years,
Keystone has provided fully
accredited, independent study
programs to high school students with
unique personal dreams, and from
many educational backgrounds. Our
students work at their own pace, make
important connections, and excel
academically, all toward achieving
their goals. Along the way, they
develop practical life skills they can
take wherever life leads them.

Eligibility: Must provide proof of
completion of eighth grade and must
be proficient in English

Online high school courses offered:

3D Animation I

3D Animation I and II

3D Animation II

Algebra 1

Algebra 2

American Government (also in
Honors)

American History

Art and Music Appreciation

Biology (also in Honors)

Business Law

Chemistry (also in Honors)

Civics (also in Honors)

Computer Fundamentals

Computer Fundamentals: Excel and
PowerPoint

Computer Fundamentals: Word,
Internet and E-Mail

Consumer Math

Creative Writing

Driver Education

Earth Science (also in Honors)

Economics (also in Honors)

English 1 (also in Honors)

English 2 (also in Honors)

English 3 (also in Honors)

English 4

Fine Art

French 1

French 2

Geography (also in Honors)

Geometry

German 1

German 2

Grammar and Composition

Health

Introduction to Technology

Life Science

Marketing

MS Office Applications, Level 1

Multimedia

Multimedia: Digital Photography and
Graphics

Multimedia: Web Design

Physical Science

Physics

continued on next page

Keystone National High School
continued from previous page

Prealgebra

Precalculus

Programming (with VisualStudio.NET)

Programming: C++ Programming

Programming: MS VisualBasic.NET

Psychology

Refresher Math

Skills for Success

Sociology

Spanish 1

Spanish 2

World History (also in Honors)

Offers diploma? Yes

Tuition: Full-time status (five courses) for $1,045 and $1,845. Individual online courses for $369 per full-credit course or $264 for a half-credit course

Accreditation: Distance Education and Training Council

Northwest Association of Accredited Schools

Laurel Springs School

P.O. Box 1440
Ojai, CA 93024-1440

Phone: Toll-free (800) 377-5890 or (805) 646-2473

Web site:
http://www.laurelsprings.com

Description: Laurel Springs School is an accredited K–12 personalized distance learning program providing a variety of curricular options, trained teachers, college counseling, grades, diplomas, and official transcripts. Using a diverse selection of approved texts and technological resources, we offer families a specialized array of educational programs in a distance learning environment.

Laurel Springs School assesses each child's learning style and assists families in choosing their educational program. Our teachers regularly consult with each of their students, providing personalized instruction tailored to maximize learning. Our students become active learners who think independently, communicate effectively, and see themselves as members of a global community.

Eligibility: Anyone may enroll.

Online high school courses offered:

Algebra 1

Algebra 2

American History

American History (Honors)

American Literature

American Literature (Honors)

Art History

Biology With lab

Biology With lab (Honors)

British Literature

Creative Writing

Design with Photoshop

Drama in Literature

Drama in Literature (Honors)

Driver's Education

Earth Science

Earth Science (Honors)

Economics

EFL – English as a Foreign Language

English – Journal Writing

English Fundamentals

English Fundamentals (Honors)

French 1

French 2

General Science

Geometry

Health

Introduction to the Internet

Life Management

Math Proficiency

Media Literacy – Fine Arts

Mythology

Oceanography

Oceanography (Honors)

Renaissance Art

SAT Prep

Shakespearean Literature

Shakespearean Literature (Honors)

Spanish 1

Spanish 2

Spanish 3

Study of the Environment

Survival Math

The Fellowship of the Ring

Trigonometry

World Cultures

World History

World History (Honors)

World Literature (Honors)

Writing Tutorials

Offers diploma? Yes

Tuition: $325 to $400 for a one-semester online course or $625 to $750 for a full-year online course.

Accreditation: National Independent Study Accreditation Council

Western Association of Schools and Colleges

Louisiana Virtual School

Louisiana Center for Educational Technology
Louisiana Department of Education
2758-D Brightside Drive
Baton Rouge, LA 70820

Phone: (225) 763-5575

Fax: (225) 763-8592

Web site:
http://www.louisianavirtualschool.net

E-mail: Ken.Bradford@LA.Gov

Description: The Louisiana Department of Education in partnership with the Louisiana School for Math, Science, and the Arts provides Louisiana high school students access to standards-based high school courses delivered by Louisiana teachers through the Louisiana Virtual School. Students in LVS courses utilize the Web, e-mail, and other online and offline resources to complete a rich course of study in a multitude of courses.

The LVS affords schools the opportunity to expand learning opportunities to students through courses that would not otherwise be available to them. Most LVS courses are offered as full-year courses following a traditional time schedule. However, some courses are offered as full-credit block courses or as half-credit semester courses.

Eligibility: Any Louisiana student who attends an approved public or nonpublic school in Louisiana is eligible. The school must be in compliance with *Brumfield vs. Dodd*. A

continued on next page

Louisiana Virtual School
continued from previous page

nonpublic school must have a sectarian questionnaire on file with the Louisiana Board of Elementary and Secondary Education.

Online high school courses offered:

A.P. American History

Advanced Math

Algebra I

American History

Astronomy

Biology I

Biology II

Calculus

Chemistry

Civics

Computer Science I

Conceptual Physics

Earth Science

English IV

Environmental Science

Fine Arts Survey

Free Enterprise

French I

French II

Geometry

Independent Study in Technology Applications

Latin I

Latin II

Spanish I

Spanish II

Spanish III

Survey of the Arts

Web Mastering

World History

Offers diploma? No

Tuition: Free to Louisiana residents. Dual-course enrollment option requires a $100 payment to Northwestern State University.

Computer requirements:

PC with Pentium II 400-MHz processor and Windows 98

64-MB RAM color monitor (16-bit, 800 x 600 resolution)

8x or faster CD-ROM drive

Internet access

Sound card, speakers, headphones, and a microphone

A current browser (IE 5.5)

Accreditation: The Louisiana Department of Education does not accredit schools as providers of distance learning. The Board of Elementary and Secondary Education has adopted the *Louisiana Standards for Distance Education.*

Maryland Virtual Learning Opportunities

Maryland State Department of Education
200 W. Baltimore Street
Baltimore, MD 21201

Phone: (410) 767-0734

Fax: (410) 333-2128

Web site:
http://www.mdk12online.org

E-mail: lglowa@msde.state.md.us

Description: Through the delivery of high-quality online courses, the

Maryland Virtual Learning Opportunities Program, an educational service managed by the Maryland State Department of Education, is designed to expand the access of Maryland public school students. We deliver challenging curricula aligned to the Maryland Content Standards as well as to other appropriate standards

MVLO offers online courses for high school credit in collaboration with local school systems. The teaching is conducted online with the teacher physically separated from the student. The teacher communicates with the student online and via the telephone, and a school site coordinator provides site-based support.

Eligibility: Students who are enrolled in and attending a Maryland public school or who are placed by the local school system in an approved nonpublic special education school placement may enroll in a MVLO course with prior approval from the local school or school system.

Online high school courses offered:

A.P. Art History

A.P. Calculus AB

A.P. Computer Science A

A.P. English Literature and Composition

A.P. Macroeconomics

A.P. Microeconomics

A.P. Physics B

A.P. Statistics

A.P. U.S. Government

Accounting 1A

Accounting 1B

Algebra and Data Analysis

Calculus

English 11: American Literature

English 12: British Literature

Geometry

Health

Introduction to HTML

Physics

U.S. Government

Offers diploma? No

Tuition: Fees are charged to the student's school district, but the district may require the parent to pay the fees.

Computer requirements:

Windows-based computers:

Windows 98, 98 SE, ME, NT, 2000, or XP

32 MB RAM (64 MB recommended)

28.8-K Internet connection (56 K recommended)

Sound card and speakers

Internet Explorer 5.0, 5.5, 6.0

Netscape Communicator 4.77, 4.78, 4.79

Macintosh computers:

Mac OS 8.1 or higher

32 MB RAM (64 MB recommended)

28.8-K Internet connection (56 K recommended)

Sound card and speakers

Internet Explorer 4.5, 5.0, 5.01

Netscape Communicator 4.77, 4.78, 4.79

Michigan Virtual High School

Michigan Virtual University
3101 Technology Parkway., Suite G
Lansing, MI 48910

Phone: Toll-free (800) 393-6052

Fax: (517) 664-5395

Web site: http://www.mivhs.org

E-mail: mvhs@mivu.org

Description: The Michigan Virtual High School is an online resource that enables Michigan high schools to provide courses and other learning tools that students wouldn't otherwise have access to. Courses are taught by Michigan certified teachers who are highly qualified in their area of expertise. The Michigan Virtual High School was first funded by the Michigan Legislature in July 2000 to be operated by the Michigan Virtual University. The Michigan Virtual University is a private nonprofit 501(c)(3) Michigan corporation governed by a board of directors representing business, education leaders, and state government.

Eligibility: Anyone may enroll.

Online high school courses offered:

A.P. Art History

A.P. Biology

A.P. Calculus

A.P. Chemistry

A.P. Computer Science

A.P. Exam Review

A.P. French

A.P. Macroeconomics

A.P. Microeconomics

A.P. Physics

A.P. Psychology

A.P. Spanish

A.P. Statistics

A.P. U.S. Government and Politics

A.P. U.S. History

Advanced Composition

Algebra

American Film Survey

American Government

American History

American Literature

Anatomy and Physiology

Art History

Astronomy

Beginning Composition

Biology

Business and Consumer Math

Business and Personal Protocol

Business Communication

Calculus

Career Planning

Chemistry

Chinese (Mandarin)

Civics

Computer Science

Earth Science

Economics

Employability Skills

English 9

English 10

English 11

English 12

Environmental Science

ESL

Essential Reading Skills

Exam Review

French

Geography

Geometry

German

Global Issues

Health Science

HTML, Dynamic HTML, and Scripting

Human Space Exploration

Intermediate Writing Process and Practice

International Business

Introduction to English Literature and Composition

Introduction to Technology

Introduction to C++

IT Basics

Journalism

Keyboarding

Latin

Legal Issues

Life and Job Skills

Macroeconomics

Math Fundamentals

Math Skills

MEA.P. Smart Curriculum

Microeconomics

Microsoft Office XP

Oceanography

Personal Economics and Finance

Physics

Prealgebra

Precalculus

Pre-College Test Review (ACT/SAT/PSAT)

Psychology

Reading Comprehension

Reading for Information

Reading Strategies

Skills for Health

Sociology

Spanish

Statistics

Study Skills

Trigonometry

U.S. Government and Politics

U.S. History

Web Design Basics HTML

World Civilizations

World History

World Literature

Offers diploma? The MVHS does not grant credit or diplomas but works in partnership with local high schools. The MVHS provides an end of course achievement percentage to the local mentor (teacher of record), who in turn translates the score into the local school district's grading scale.

Tuition: The MVHS has structured courses to best fit the needs of the student's learning style. There are four different course formats or structures that the MVHS offers: Advanced Placement, Flex 90, Semester Paced, and Student Direct. Courses range from $129 to $350 per course.

Computer requirements:

A fast, reliable Internet connection

E-mail

Our Web pages display best at a screen resolution of 800 x 600 pixels and a

continued on next page

Michigan Virtual High School
continued from previous page

color depth of Hi Color (16-bit/64 K) or greater. Using these settings will require less vertical scrolling and improve the appearance of graphics.

Your computer's speed and the amount of system and video memory are important. A Pentium-speed PC or Power Mac with at least 32 MB will significantly improve your interactive learning experience. Additional hardware such as a CD-ROM and/or sound card (with speakers or headphones) may be required for some MVHS courses.

Accreditation: Accreditation candidacy status from the Commission on International and Trans-Regional Accreditation

Milwaukee Area Technical College

700 W. State Street
Milwaukee, WI 53233-1443

Phone: (414) 297-7987

Web site:
http://www.matc.edu/student/offerings/precollege/online.html

E-mail: mulvennk@matc.edu

Description: The online diploma program offers high school classes for credit online. Staffed by a caring and committed faculty who have been selected for their experience and innovative approaches to learning, the program makes instruction available at any time and in any place convenient to the student. Those students who may not own or have access to a computer can take advantage of computer labs at any one of four MATC regional campuses.

Eligibility: Anyone may enroll. Those between the ages of 16 and 18 must have written permission from a counselor or other school official.

Online high school courses offered: In any given semester, you can take online courses in communication, English, mathematics, health, history, natural sciences, social sciences, and more.

Offers diploma? Yes

Tuition: $20 to $25 per credit for Wisconsin residents.

Minnesota Center of Online Learning

306 W. Elm Street
Houston, MN 55943

Phone: (507) 896-5323 option 4

Fax: (507) 896-4757

Web site: http://www.mcool.org

E-mail:
steve.kerska@houston.k12.mn.us

Description: The Minnesota Center of Online Learning (MCoOL) is a web-based learning resource designed to meet the educational needs of Minnesota public school students and educators. All courses provided by MCoOL are taught by Minnesota licensed teachers to provide the best educational experience possible.

Eligibility: Limited to Minnesota residents between 9th and 12th grade.

Online high school courses offered:

Advanced Composition

Algebra 1

Algebra 2

American Government

American History 1

American Literature

Anthropology

Archeology

Art

Beginning Composition

Biology

Business and Personal Protocol

Business and Consumer Math

Business and Consumer Math

Business Communication

Career Planning

Chemistry 1A

Civics

Creative Writing

Geometry

Health Science

International Business

Introduction to Psychology

Introduction to Technology

Keyboarding

Life Fitness

Life Science Oceanography

Macroeconomics

Math Skills Review

Personal Economics and Finance

Physical Science

Physics

Prealgebra

Precalculus

Reading Comprehension

Spanish 1

Spanish 2

Web Site Building

World Civilizations

World Literature

Offers diploma? Yes

Tuition: None for public school students. Others pay tuition.

Computer requirements:

Pentium-class PC with Windows 95 or higher, Macintosh with OS 8.5 or higher.

64 MB RAM

Color monitor with 16-bit, 800 x 600 resolution

8x or faster CD-ROM drive

Keyboard and mouse

Direct network connection or 56-K modem with Internet access

Sound card and speakers

Hard disk with at least 40 MB available

Netscape Communicator 4.61 or higher, or Microsoft Internet Explorer 5.0 or higher (available on your provided course CD)

QuickTime 4.0, Flash 5.0, and Authorware plug-ins (available on your provided course CD)

Minnesota Online High School

University Technology Center
1313 Fifth Street, SE
Minneapolis, MN 55414

Phone: (612) 227-8499

Fax: (866) 586-2870

Web site: http://www.mnohs.org

E-mail: info@mnohs.org

continued on next page

Minnesota Online High School
continued from previous page

Description: Minnesota Online High School (MNOHS) was started by a core group of four educators who have worked together in online education since 1996, having founded one of the first online high school programs in the country. Members of the development team are recognized as pioneers in the field of online high school learning, and MNOHS grew out of their combined experience.

The mission of MNOHS is to combine proven educational strategies with the wonderful flexibility of online learning. The staff and faculty at MNOHS believe that online education can and should be a highly interactive, academically and socially rich experience for all students. They are dedicated to educating the whole student and to creating a thriving, diverse educational community. MNOHS provides a full range of student support services aimed at helping students research a variety of career paths and explore their options for financing and attending college. The curriculum emphasizes college readiness skills, including solid reading, writing, math and critical thinking skills. MNOHS also prepares students to use online tools such as threaded discussions, whiteboards, shared calendars, online interactive textbooks, and instant messaging that are currently being integrated into traditional college classes. Graduates of MNOHS will understand their career and college options and will have the tools for success.

Eligibility: The school serves students up to age 21 in grades 10 through 12 (10th-grade classes will be added for the 2006–2007 school year). Tuition is free for Minnesota residents. Residents of other states or citizens of other countries may be eligible to participate for a tuition fee (to be determined).

Online high school courses offered:

Directed Studies: Health Issues and Choices

Directed Studies: Music

Directed Studies: Theater

Algebra 1

Algebra 2

American Literature

Basic Skills

Biology

British Literature

Career and Educational Exploration

Chemistry

Earth Science

Economics

Geometry

Government

Prealgebra

Research Learning

Spanish 1

Spanish 2

U.S. History

Visual Arts

World Literature

Offers diploma? Yes

Tuition: Free to Minnesota residents. Residents of other states or citizens of other countries are charged a tuition fee (to be determined).

Computer requirements:

Pentium II (233 MHz minimum, higher recommended)

Internet connection of at least 56 K (broadband recommended)

Windows 98, 2000, NT, XP

256 MB RAM

12x CD-ROM

Monitor screen resolution of 1024 x 768

Printer required

A way to save work to a removable disk (floppy drive, Zip drive, or the capability to write to a CD)

A sound card with speakers or headset

Accreditation: MNOHS is a public charter school and an approved online learning program in the state of Minnesota. MNOHS has begun the accreditation process.

Mississippi Online Learning Institute

Office of Educational Technology
359 N. West Street
Jackson, MS 39205

Phone: (601) 359-3954

Web site: http://molli.mde.k12.ms.us

E-mail: merobinson@mde.k12.ms.us

Description: Mississippi Online Learning Institute is a Web-based educational service offered by the Mississippi Department of Education to provide Mississippi students and educators with access to a wider range of course work, with more flexibility in scheduling, and with the opportunity to develop their capacities as independent learners.

Eligibility: High school students from Mississippi are eligible to enroll.

Online high school courses offered:

A.P. American Government

A.P. Calculus AB

A.P. English Language and Composition

A.P. English Literature and Composition

A.P. European History

A.P. French Language

A.P. Macroeconomics

A.P. Microeconomics

A.P. Physics

A.P. Spanish Language

Algebra 2

American Government

Economics

International Business

Personal Economics and Finance

Principles of CAD

Psychology

Psychology – Training

Spanish I

Web Page Design

Offers diploma? No

Tuition: $550 per semester course or $750 for a full-year course. The student's school district may pay the fee or require the student to do so.

Computer requirements:

Windows-based computers:

Windows 95, 98, NT, or later

90-MHz Pentium Processor

32 MB RAM

continued on next page

Mississippi Online Learning Institute
continued from previous page

28.8-K modem

Sound card

Speakers

RealPlayer Basic

Updated Browser with QuickTime

Macintosh computers:

Mac OS 8.1 or later

604 PowerPC processor

32 MB RAM

28.8-K modem

Speakers

RealPlayer Basic

Updated browser with QuickTime

Missouri Virtual School

Missouri State University
901 S. National Avenue
Springfield, MO 65804

Phone: (417) 836-4743

Fax: (417) 836-4266

Web site: http://mvs.smsu.edu

E-mail: mvs@smsu.edu

Description: The mission of the Missouri Virtual School is to serve the educational needs of all students through virtual learning communities. Students register through their local school.

Eligibility: Students in Missouri may register.

Online high school courses offered:

A.P. Calculus AB

A.P. Creative Writing

A.P. Economics, Micro

A.P. U.S. Government and Politics

A.P. U.S. History

American Literature

Analytic Geometry and Calculus I

Basic Astronomy with Laboratory

College Algebra

Computers for Learning

Conceptual Physics

Creative Writing

French I

French II

French III

French IV

Fundamentals of Chemistry

Intermediate Algebra

Introduction to Physics

Introduction to Tropical Marine Science

Precalculus

Principles of Biological Science

Spanish I

Spanish II

Spanish III

Spanish IV

Trigonometry

Offers diploma? No. The local school district awards the high school credit.

Tuition: The student's school district is billed.

Computer requirements:

Windows 98, 2000 (SP1), or XP

Internet Explorer 5.x, 6.x, or Netscape 4.5x, 4.7x, 7.x

28.8-K (or faster) Internet connection

350-MHz (or faster) processor

128 MB RAM (or more) of memory

40 MB (or more) free space on hard drive

Monitor with 16-bit colors (high color)

Sound card, headset with microphone

Monroe Virtual High School

1220 16th Avenue
Monroe, WI 53566

Phone: Toll-free (888) 947-6437 or (608) 328-7007

Fax: (608) 328-7288

Web site:
http://www.virtualdiploma.net

E-mail:
virtual.school@monroe.k12.wi.us

Description: The Monroe Virtual High School (MVHS) offers a unique and flexible approach to earning high school credit using computer-based courses, correspondence, and experiential credit-based options. The program is approved by the School District of Monroe Board of Education and offers a four-year high school diploma. The MVHS program is based on the belief that all students have the right to the opportunity to earn a high school diploma, while recognizing that not all students are able to accomplish this in a traditional educational setting.

Eligibility: Anyone may enroll.

Online high school courses offered:

A.P. Art History

A.P. Biology

A.P. Calculus AB

A.P. English Language and

Composition

A.P. English Literature and Composition

A.P. Government and Politics

A.P. Macroeconomics

A.P. Microeconomics

A.P. U.S. History

Accounting

Adult Roles and Responsibilities

Advanced Algebra

Advanced Grammar and Composition

Aerospace: Crossing the Space Frontier

African-American Literature

AgriScience

Algebra Level I

Algebra Level II

American Government

American Government: National Level

American Government: Theories, Policies and Politics

American History

American History Since 1898

American History to 1898

American Literature

American Literature Studies

American Literature: Society and Developing Identities

The American Short Story

Ancient Egyptian Civilization

Anthropology

Applied Math

Art I

Art Appreciation

continued on next page

Monroe Virtual High School
continued from previous page

Art History and Appreciation (Art History)

Astronomy

Basic Art

Basic Composition

Basic Electricity and Electronics

Basic Expository Writing

Basic Grammar

Basic Mathematics

Basic Vocabulary

Beginning Accounting

Beginning Food and Nutrition

Beginning Piano

The Bible as Literature (Biblical Literature)

Biology 2

Biology I/Honors

Biology Level I

Business and Consumer Mathematics

Business and International Etiquette

Business and Personal Law

Business Communications (Technical/Business Communication)

Business English and Communication

Business Law

Business Mathematics

Business Systems Technology

Calculus

Career Explorations

Career Planning

Chemistry 1 (With Lab)

Chemistry 1 (Without Lab)

Chemistry 2 (With Lab)

Chemistry 2 (Without Lab)

Child Development

Civics

Clothing and Textiles

Comparative Politics

Composition with Grammar Review

Computer Applications

Computer Literacy

Computer Programming Basic

Conservation of Our Natural Resources

Consumer Economics

Consumer Education and Economics

Creative Writing

Creative Writing: Fiction

Critical Thinking

Developmental Reading

Drawing and Composition

Drawing and Storytelling (Drawing)

Driver Education

Earth-Space Science

Economics

Economics: Making Decisions

Effective Methods of Study

Effective Reader Skills

Effective Speech Communication

Elements of Interior Design

Emergent Computer Technologies

English 9th Grade

English 10th Grade

English 11th Grade

English 12th Grade

English I/Honors

English II/Honors

English III/Honors

English IV/Honors

English Literature

English Literature Through Shakespeare

Entrepreneurship

Environmental Science

Ethnic Studies and Human Relations

The Experience of Drama (Dramatic Literature)

Family and Personal Etiquette

Family Health Care

First Year Algebra

Fitness for Well-Being

Fitness Lifestyle Design

Five Novels of Change

Foods and Nutrition

French I

French II

French III

General Business

General Homemaking: Clothing and Foods

General Homemaking: Home Management

General Mathematics

General Shop

Geometry

German I

German II

German III

Global Studies

Grammar, Spelling, and Vocabulary

Health Education

Health Science

Her Stories: Women's Voices in American Literature

Horticulture, Landscaping

Horticulture, Lawn and Plant Care

Housing and Interior Design

Housing Decisions

Improving Reading and Study Skills

Indians of Missouri

Integrated Mathematics

Intermediate Grammar

Intermediate Piano

Interpersonal Relationships

Introduction to Black and White Photography

Introduction to Business

Introduction to Computer Programming: Visual Basic

Introduction to Computers and Information Technology

Introduction to Driving

Introduction to High School Journalism

Introduction to Human Relations

Introduction to Marketing (Marketing Foundations)

Introduction to Mass Media Studies

Introduction to Nutrition

Introduction to Personal and Social Psychology

Introduction to Poetry

Introductory Earth and Space Science Level I

Introductory Horticulture

Introductory Photography

Japanese I

Journalism

Keyboarding/Typewriting

continued on next page

Monroe Virtual High School
continued from previous page

King Arthur and the Middle Ages

Latin I

Latin II

Latin III

Law in America

Library Skills and Research (Library Media)

Life Management Skills

Literature of the Future (Themes in Literature)

Marine Science I

Marketing

Mass Media

Mathematics of Money

Medieval History

Missouri History

Multicultural Literature

Music Appreciation

Music Theory

Mysteries (Genres of Literature)

Mystery Fiction

Mythology (Genres of Literature)

Office Systems

Parenting and Child Development

Personal Adjustment and Family Living

Personal Adjustment, Dating and Marriage

Personal Finance

Personal Finance and Economic Practices

Personal Fitness

Personal Keyboarding

Physical Science

Physical Science: An Introduction to Chemistry

Physical Science: An Introduction to Physics

Physics 1

Physics 2

Planning for College

Precalculus

Principles of Art

Principles of Marketing

Project Self-Discovery (Vocational Information)

Psychology

Psychology: Foundations of Human Behavior

Readings in Science Fiction

Readings in the American Novel

Readings in the Short Story

Research: Process and Presentation

Science Fiction for Reluctant Readers

Search for Identity Through Literature

Second Year French

Second-Year Latin

Senior-Year Composition (Advanced Composition)

Short Stories for Reluctant Readers

The Short Story (Short Stories)

Small-Engine Care and Operation

Small-Engine Maintenance and Repair

Societal Issues in a Contemporary World

Sociology

Spanish Level I

Spanish Level II

Spanish Level III

Speak Your Mind: A Guide to Clear Thinking and Communication

Special Topics in Geology

Speech

Statistics

Studying in College and Other Places (Basic Skills Development)

Studying Planet Earth: The Satellite Connection

Trigonometry

The Underground World of Caves

Understanding and Improving Your Memory (Basic Skills Development)

U.S. Government

U.S. History

Vocabulary for the College-Bound Student

Vocational Information (Career Information and Exploration)

Web Design 1

Women Writers: Fiction and Autobiography (Themes in Literature)

World Cultures

World Geography

World History

World History Since the American Revolution

World History to the American Revolution

World Religions

Writing for Beginners

You and the Law

Offers diploma? Yes

Tuition: Free to Wisconsin residents.

Accreditation: North Central Association of Colleges and Schools

The MorningStar Academy

10151 University Boulevard, Suite 334 Orlando, FL 32817-1904

Phone: Toll-free (866) STUDY 2004

Web site: http://www. themorningstaracademy.org

E-mail: StudentServices@TheMorningStarAcademy.org

Description: The MorningStar Academy is a registered and accredited private online school. MorningStar offers over 110 K–12 God-centered, teacher-led courses, all with the flexibility of homeschooling. High school students can also earn their diploma in the comfort of their own home.

Eligibility: Anyone may enroll.

Online high school courses offered:

A.P. Biology

A.P. English Language

A.P. English Literature

A.P. European History

A.P. French Language

A.P. U.S. History

Bible 9: New Testament

Bible 10: Old Testament

Bible 11: Authentic Christian Living

Bible 12: Solid Ground Theology

Christian Evangelism

Christian Fantasy and Fiction

Christian Manhood

Christian Womanhood

Cinema History

Creative Writing

continued on next page

The MorningStar Academy
continued from previous page

Discovering God's Creation Science: Science 9–12: Biology

Discovering God's Creation Science: Science 10–12: Chemistry

Discovering God's Creation Science: Science 11–12: Physics

Driver's Education

English 9: Creative Composition

English 10: Writing with Wisdom

English 11: Exploration and Expression

English 12: Celebrating the Classics

French 1

French 2

German 1

Introduction to Business

Introduction to Law

Introduction to Psychology

Introduction to Sociology

Journalism

Latin 1

Life Skills

Math 7–12: Algebra 1

Math 7–12: Algebra 1 With Saxon

Math 8–12: Geometry

Math 8–12: Integrated 1

Math 9–12: Algebra 2

Math 9–12: Algebra 2 with Saxon

Math 9–12: Consumer Math

Math 10–12: Trigonometry

Math 11–12: Calculus

Media Arts

Music: 20th Century Music

Music: Art and Music 9–12: Continuing Your Exploration

Music: Christian Symbolism in Fine Art

Music: History of Christian Music

Music: Music Studio

SAT, College and Career Preparation

Social Action

Social Studies 9–12: Government and Economics

Social Studies 10–12: World History

Social Studies 11–12: World Religions

Spanish 1

Spanish 2

Video Game Development

Video Studio

Web Design

Wonderfully Made Health and Physical Education: Health and Physical Education 9–12: Dealing With Dangers

Offers diploma? Yes

Tuition: $1,800 (early enrollment discounts available)

Computer requirements:

Pentium III processor

256 KB RAM

6-GB hard drive

Floppy drive

CD-ROM drive

56-K modem or faster

Windows 98 or higher

We highly suggest a printer.

Accreditation: National Private Schools Accreditation Alliance

National University Virtual High School

11355 N. Torrey Pines Road
La Jolla, CA 92037-1011

Phone: Toll-free (866) 366-8847

Fax: (858) 642-8750

Web site: http://www.nuvhs.org

E-mail: info@nuvhs.org

Description: NUVHS students complete a full semester course in only eight weeks, with five eight-week sessions per year. This accelerated format allows students to focus their energies on just a few subjects at a time while covering all curricula required in an academic year. Classes will begin each September, November, January, March, and at the end of June. This model allows students who may be failing a class mid-semester in their traditional school an opportunity to complete the course at NUVHS and to keep them on track for graduation.

Eligibility: Anyone may enroll.

Online high school courses offered:

A.P. Biology A/B

A.P. Chemistry A/B

A.P. European History A/B

A.P. Government

A.P. Psychology A

A.P. U.S. History A

Advanced Digital Photography

Algebra I A/B

Algebra II A/B

American Government

Biology A/B

Calculus A/B/C

Chemistry A/B

Economics

English 9 A/B

English 10 A/B (World Literature)

English 11 A/B (American Literature)

English 12 A/B (British Literature)

Game Theory

Geometry A/B

Health

Introduction to Computers

Introduction to Digital Photography

Introduction to Journalism

Marine Science A/B

Nutrition and Weight Management

Prealgebra A/B

Precalculus A/B

Spanish I A/B

Spanish II A/B

Sports Training

U.S. History A/B

World History A/B

Offers diploma? Yes

Tuition: $600 for a semester-length course

Computer requirements:

Windows-based computers:

Microsoft Windows, Windows 98, 98 SE, ME, NT, 2000, or XP

64 MB RAM (128 recommended)

28.8-K modem (56 K or better recommended)

Sound card and speakers

Microphone (or headset)

continued on next page

National University Virtual High School
continued from previous page

Macintosh computers:
8.0–9.1 (OS X 10.1 in "classic mode")
(OS X 10.2 (Jaguar) compatibility is currently being tested)
32 MB RAM (64 or 128 recommended)
28.8-K modem (56 K or better recommended)
Sound card and speakers
Microphone (or headset)

New Jersey Virtual School

100 Tornillo Way
Tinton Falls, NJ 07712
Phone: (732) 389-5555 ext. 1000
Fax: (732) 542-0302
Web site: http://www.njvs.org
E-mail: njvhs@moesc.org
Description: With the New Jersey Virtual School, no longer do students have to be subject to rigid definitions of time and place. The New Jersey Virtual School empowers you to become educated utilizing the freedom of the Internet. Earn your credits where you want and when you want.
Eligibility: Anyone may enroll.
Online high school courses offered:
A.P. Biology
A.P. Computer Science A
A.P. English Literature
A.P. Microeconomics
A.P. Physics
Algebra I
Algebra II
Biology
Chemistry
English I
English II
English III
English IV
Geometry
Latin I
Latin II
Marine Science
Physical Education
Physics
SAT Preparation
Spanish I
U.S. History I
U.S. History II
World History
Offers diploma? Yes
Tuition: $350 to $800
Computer requirements:
PC with Pentium II processor and Windows 98 or higher, or Macintosh with PowerPC processor and System 8.5 or higher.
64 MB RAM
Color monitor (16-bit color and 800 x 600 resolution)
8x or faster CD-ROM drive
Direct network connection or 56-K modem with Internet access
Sound card and speakers
Hard drive with at least 40 MB available
A current browser (Netscape Communicator 4.61 or higher, or Microsoft Internet Explorer 5.0 or higher)

North Dakota Division of Independent Study

Box 5036
Fargo, ND 58105-5036

Phone: (701) 231-6000

Fax: (701) 231-6052

Web site:
http://www.dis.dpi.state.nd.us

E-mail: ndis.enroll@sendit.nodak.edu

Description: The mission of the Division of Independent Study is to provide a delivery system of distance education curricula in a manner consistent with sound educational practices. Courses may be started at any time. Courses are to be completed within 12 months.

Eligibility: Anyone may enroll.

Online high school courses offered:

A.P. Human Geography

Alcohol, Tobacco, and Other Drugs

Algebra

American Government

American Literature

Auto Fundamentals

Biology

British Literature

Business English

Business Use – Computers

Character Education

Chemistry

Child Development

The Classic Novel

College Algebra

Computer Applications

Consumer Math

Creative Writing

Current Events

Developmental English

Digital Photography

Driver Education

Economics

Elementary Algebra

Environmental Science

First Aid

Fitness for Life

French

Freshman Language and Composition

Freshman Literature

Fundamentals of Public Speaking

Fundamentals of Music

General Math

Geometry

Global Politics

Health

Individual and Team Sports

Intermediate Algebra

Junior Language and Composition

Knowing About Art

Law and Justice

Literature for Reluctant Readers

Local History

Microcomputer Packages

Modern World History

Mythology

Personal Finance

Personal Management

Physical Science

Physics

Project Self-Discovery – Psychology

continued on next page

North Dakota Division of Independent Study
continued from previous page

Relationships

Senior Language and Composition

Sociology

Sophomore Language and Composition

Sophomore Literature

Spanish

Trigonometry

U.S. History

Wildlife Management

World Geography

World History

Offers diploma? Yes

Tuition: North Dakota residents are charged $88 for a semester-long course. Nonresidents are charged $97.

Accreditation: Commission on International and Trans-Regional Accreditation

North Central Association Commission on Accreditation and School Improvement

Northern Star Online

Intermediate District 287
1820 Xenium Lane N.
Plymouth, MN 55441-3790

Phone: (763) 559-3535

Fax: (763) 550-7199

Web site:
http://www.northernstaronline.org

E-mail:
registrar@northernstaronline.org

Description: Northern Star Online is a collaborative of seven independent school districts and two educational service agencies. Building on course work developed by each of the partners, the collaboration has been created to further the state of Minnesota's goal of promoting high-quality online learning.

Eligibility: Anyone may register, but the focus is on grades 9 through 12.

Online high school courses offered:

A.P. Macroeconomics

A.P. Microeconomics

A.P. Statistics

Advanced American History

Advanced Middle Math I (test information required for enrollment)

Advanced Middle Math II (test information required for enrollment)

Advanced Web Design

Algebra I

Algebra II

American Literature

Astronomy

Biology

Core IIA (9)

Core IIIA (10)

Emotional Intelligence

English 9

Exploring Geometry

Functions: Statistics and Trigonometry

Government 9

Health Science

Independent Living

Introduction to Child Development

Introduction to Computer Science

Introduction to Horticulture
Introduction to Psychology I
Introduction to Psychology II
Japanese I
Latin I
Physical Education
Science 9
Sports/Entertainment Marketing
Technical Careers Exploration
U.S. History I
U.S. History II
World Studies
Writing Process

Offers diploma? No. Courses can be used by Minnesota students to receive academic credit that meets the Minnesota state academic standards.

Tuition: Free to Minnesota public school students. Others pay tuition.

Computer requirements:

A Macintosh computer running OS 8.6 or higher (9.1 or higher strongly recommended) or a PC-compatible computer, Pentium II (266 MHz) or better, running Win 95/98 or higher

Microphone and speakers (or headset) providing audio in and out capability

Internet connection (56-K modem, cable modem, or DSL)

128 MB installed RAM (more RAM is strongly recommended on both platforms)

Hard disk space for downloading files and work in progress

Microsoft Internet Explorer 5 or higher

Java for Mac OS

MRJ 2.2.5 or higher
QuickTime 5.0 or higher
Flash Player
Adobe Acrobat Reader 5.0 or higher
WebStart or WebLauncher, which runs the software necessary to access the required online chat sessions

Other software—such as a word processing program or plug-ins for your browser—may be required by individual courses for completing course assignments.

Accreditation: Courses are approved by the Minnesota Department of Education and meet state academic standards. Instructors are licensed Minnesota teachers.

NorthStar Academy

6145 Lehman Drive, Suite 100
Colorado Springs, CO 80918

Phone: Toll-free (888) 464-6280 or (719) 268-0116

Fax: (719) 531-7618

Web site: http://www.northstar-academy.org

E-mail: info@northstar-academy.org

Description: NorthStar Academy is a community of learners in an online school. It uses the Internet to link students with other students and accredited teachers who provide 100% of the students' instruction and marking. Through the conferencing software called FirstClass, teachers send their lessons and assignments over the Internet, lead group discussions, evaluate students'

continued on next page

North Star Academy
continued from previous page

assignments, and engage in most of the same teacher-student interactions that occur in traditional classrooms. Students complete their assigned work using printed material and software provided by the school. Completed assignments and exams are sent back to teachers for marking and then returned to the students via e-mail. Operates on an August-to-June schedule.

Eligibility: Anyone may enroll.

Online high school courses offered:

A.P. Biology

A.P. Calculus

A.P. Chemistry

A.P. Computer Science 1 – JAVA

A.P. Economics – Micro

A.P. World History

Accounting

Advanced Creative Writing

Algebra 1

Algebra 2

Biology

British Literature

Business Math

Career Planning

Chemistry

College Preparation

Computer Science – Introduction

Creative Writing

Cultural Immersion

Electronics

Expository Writing

Geometry

Grammar and Style

Greek Mythology

Health Education 110

Humanities 1

Humanities 2

Isaiah and the Bible

Isaiah and Creation Keyboarding

Language Arts 9

Latin 1

Latin 2

Learning Office 3

Logic 1

Logic 2

Music Appreciation

New Testament Survey

Old Testament Survey

Physical Education 100

Physics

Precalculus

SAT preparation

Science 9

Science 10

Spanish 1

Spanish 2

U.S. Economics (Cox)

U.S. Government

U.S. History 101 (Colonial through Civil War)

U.S. History 102 (Reconstruction to Present)

U.S. Literature

Web page Design – Intermediate

Web page Design – Introduction

Western Civilization

World Geography

World Literature

World Views in Conflict

Offers diploma? Yes

Tuition: $290 for a one-semester class or $490 for a two-semester class

Computer requirements:

Power Mac with OS 8.6 or newer or Pentium with Windows 98 or newer. Web design classes require a Pentium 3 (600 MHz) running at least Windows 98 or a G3 (500 MHz) running OS X on a Macintosh

CD player

2-GB hard disk

128 MB RAM

Modem (28.8 K or faster)

Internet connection

Printer

Scanner

VCR and cassette tape player for some courses

Microsoft Office (version 97 or newer)

DVD player

Accreditation: Northwest Association of Accredited Schools

Oak Meadow School

P.O. Box 1346
Brattleboro, VT 05302

Phone: (802) 251-7250

Fax: (802) 251-7258

Web site: http://www.oakmeadow.com

E-mail: info@oakmeadow.com

Description: In Oak Meadow High School, we believe that excellence involves more than just academics.

For students to express their innate genius, intellectual development must be balanced with self-awareness, critical thinking, interpersonal skills, and leadership qualities. The Oak Meadow curriculum encourages integrative thinking, a wide range of activities, and opportunities to do something of significance. Oak Meadow teachers seek to establish vital relationships with students, providing them with encouragement and support, and helping them to connect their academic pursuits with real-life issues and opportunities.

Eligibility: Anyone may enroll.

Online high school courses offered:

Advanced Mathematics

Algebra I

Algebra II

American Literature

Applied Business Math

Biology with Lab

Bookkeeping

Calculus

Chemistry

Consumer Mathematics

English 9

English 10

Environmental Science

French I

French II

French III

Geometry

Health/Anatomy and Physiology

Integrated Drawing

Latin I

continued on next page

Oak Meadow School
continued from previous page

Latin II

Latin III

Physics

Psychology

Spanish I

Spanish II

Spanish III

The Study of Art

U.S. Government

U.S. History

World History

World Literature

Offers diploma? Yes

Tuition: Enrollment fee of $425 per family. Teacher fees of $315 per subject.

Accreditation: Commission on International and Trans-Regional Accreditation

Commission on Secondary and Middle Schools (a commission of the Southern Association of Colleges and Schools)

On Line Academy

345 E. Prospect Avenue
Monte Vista, CO 81144

Phone: (719) 852-3951

Web site: http://monte.k12.co.us/ola

E-mail: mrmac@monte.k12.co.us

Description: OLA is the first and most experienced online school in Colorado. We offer students anywhere in Colorado a rigorous curriculum taught by highly qualified, experienced teachers. We understand that not all students fit the traditional school mold, and we are pleased to offer a positive choice to those unique students still searching for an effective way to meet their educational needs.

Eligibility: Anyone may enroll, although Colorado law limits access by homeschooled students.

Online high school courses offered:

Algebra I

Algebra II

Astronomy

Biology I

Biology II

Chemistry

Civil and Criminal Law

The Civil War in Depth

Computer and Internet Literacy

Consumer Economics

Consumer Math

Creative Writing

Earth Science

English I

English II

English III

English IV

Geometry

Health

Human Anatomy and Physiology

Introduction to Economics

Keyboarding

Life Science

Media Today

Movie Review

Physical Education

Physical Science

Prealgebra

Precalculus

Science Research Seminar

Spanish I

Spanish II

Trigonometry

U.S. History

Work Study

Offers diploma? Yes

Tuition: No charge to Colorado students who register by October. Others are charged tuition.

Computer requirements:

Pentium 4, 1.4GHz

256 RAM

20- to 40-GB hard drive

Windows XP

CD-ROM

56-K modem

Oregon Online

Southern Oregon ESD
101 N. Grape Street
Medford, OR 97501

Phone: Toll-free (800) 636-7453 or (541) 858-6723

Web site:
http://www2.soesd.k12.or.us/it/o2

E-mail:
virginia_petitt@soesd.k12.or.us

Description: The mission of Oregon Online is to provide an alternative anytime/anywhere learning opportunity for all high school students. Online learning is proving to be a compelling environment for a significant segment of our school population. The skills acquired to learn and communicate online are lifelong skills that will serve students in high school, college, and the workplace.

Eligibility: Anyone may enroll.

Online high school courses offered:

Algebra

American History

American Literature

Art History

Biology

Career Options

Chemistry

Economics

English

Geometry

Health

Personal Finance

Physical Science

Physics

Prealgebra

Precalculus

Spanish

Trigonometry

U.S. Government

World Cultures

World History

World Lit

Tuition: Oregon Online charges $300 per course per semester. However, students attending schools in districts that are members of Oregon Online receive a considerable discount. Some school districts require students to pay

continued on next page

Oregon Online
continued from previous page

for their own course; others require a deposit; others pay the entire cost.

Computer requirements:

Windows 98, ME, 2000 with all current updates

Internet Explorer 6

500-MHz Processor

128 MB RAM

CD-ROM

56-K modem with Internet connection

OSU K–12 Online

OSU Extended Campus
4943 The Valley Library
Corvallis, OR 97330

Phone: Toll-free (800) 235-6559

Fax: (541) 737-2734

Web site:
http://k12online.oregonstate.edu

E-mail: ecampus@oregonstate.edu

Description: OSU K–12 Online is a flexible learning program that currently includes approximately 35 high school classes. Curriculum includes subject areas such as English, math, science, social science, arts, health, technology, and career learning. Some courses are available on a nine-week, fast-track option. OSU Extended Campus can help schools and districts by collaborating on creating courses and programs tailored to meet students' needs.

Eligibility: Anyone may enroll.

Online high school courses offered:

A.P. Biology

Advanced Television Production

Algebra I

American History

Career Learning and Preparation

College Awareness and Career Preparation

Consumer Finance

Conversational Cultural Spanish

Creative Writing Part 1 and Part 2

Dating, Marriage and Family

Geometry

Government and Politics: United States

Health I

Independent Study: English

International Studies

Introduction to Art

Journalism

Life Science Part 1: Wildlife and Forestry of Oregon

Marine Science

Prealgebra

Spanish I

Spanish II

U.S. Government: Constitution

Web Design

Offers diploma? No

Tuition: $290 per class

Computer requirements:

Macintosh: 300 MHz or newer processor, OS 8.6 or higher, 500 MB hard drive, 128 MB RAM, 15-inch color monitor, stereo speakers or headphones (recommended), inkjet or laser printer, 56-K Internet connection (DSL or cable preferred).

Windows: Pentium II, Windows 98 or higher, 500-MB hard drive, 128 MB RAM, 15-inch color monitor, stereo speakers or headphones (recommended), inkjet or laser printer, 56-K Internet connection (DSL or cable preferred).

Unix: 500-MB hard drive, 128 MB RAM, 15-inch color monitor, stereo speakers or headphones (recommended), inkjet or laser printer, 56-K Internet connection (DSL or cable preferred).

PA LEARNERS Online Regional Cyber Charter School

475 E. Waterfront Drive
Homestead, PA 15120

Phone: (412) 394-5733

Fax: (412) 394-4604

Web site:
http://www.palearnersonline.net

E-mail: PALO@aiu3.net

Description: PA LEARNERS Online Regional Cyber Charter School (PALO) is a nonprofit, online, Web-based public school for learners across Pennsylvania. PALO provides students with 24/7 access to Blackboard, Novel Stars, Aleks, Class.com, and online textbooks. In addition, PALO uses Centra to provide real-time learning situations, which enables teachers and students to interact, assists in the tutoring of students, and allows for further explanation of concepts and ideas presented in the course material.

Eligibility: Pennsylvania residents are eligible.

Online high school courses offered:

Algebra I

Algebra II

American Government

American History

American Literature

Anthropology

Art Appreciation

Art Exploration

Astronomy

Biology

Biz Tech

British Literature

Business Math

Calculus

Career Planning

Chemistry

Civics

Earth Science

Ecology

English I

English II

Environmental Science

French

Geography

Geometry

Health

HTML Web Design

Introduction to Technology

Life Science

Math Skills Review

Modern Cultures

continued on next page

PA LEARNERS Online Regional Cyber Charter School
continued from previous page

Music

Oceanography

Pennsylvania History

Personal and Family Living

Personal Economics and Finance

Physical Education

Physical Science

Physics

Prealgebra

Precalculus

Psychology

Science Inquiry

Spanish I

Spanish II

Structure of Writing

Study Skills

World Civilizations

World Literature

Offers diploma? Yes

Tuition: Free

Pennsylvania Cyber Charter School

900 Midland Avenue
Midland, PA 15059

Phone: Toll-free (888) PACYBER (888-722-9237) or (724) 643-1180

Fax: (724) 643-2791

Web site: http://www.pacyber.org

E-mail: GeneralInfo@pacyber.org

Description: The Pennsylvania Cyber Charter School provides a free and appropriate course of study to the children of Pennsylvania families using high-quality, accredited courses of study, certified teachers, and state-of-the-art technology. PA Cyber has established the highest standards of student achievement and educational standards using both technology and regular contact between students, parents, and staff.

PA Cyber offers real-time classes with live instructors utilizing a software program, Interwise, and the Internet, thus creating the virtual classroom (VC). VC is available for students in grades 3 through 12. VC offers the flexibility of arranging a schedule, live teacher instruction, as well as independent work. VC students interact with teacher as well as classmates by spoken, written, and auditory communication. Classes meet several hours a week for instruction and have independent assignments, tests, and quizzes to complete on noninstructional days.

PA Cyber offers the Early College Program to help a student get a head start on the college experience while still enrolled in high school. We offer college-level classes to qualified high school students, allowing for both high school and college credit.

Eligibility: Must be a Pennsylvania resident.

Online high school courses offered:

Accounting

Aerospace: Crossing the Space Frontier

African-American Literature

Algebra I

Algebra II

American Government

American History

American Literature

Ancient Egyptian Civilization

Art Appreciation

Art History: From Cave to Modern Art

Basic Microsoft Office Skills

Biology

British Literature

Business and Personal Law

Business Law

Business Mathematics

Business Writing

Calculus

Career Explorations

Career Planning: Starting your Future

Changing Language: A Historical Look at English

Chemistry

Civics

Classical Mythology

Clothing and Textiles

Comparative Politics

Conservation of Our Natural Resources

Consumer Economics

Creative Writing

Criminal and Consumer Law

Critical Thinking

Cyber Basics

Earth Science

Economics

English 9

English 10

English 11

English 12

Environmental Science

Explore the Milky Way

French 1

French 2

French 3

French 4

General Biology

Geometry

German 1

German 2

German 3/4

Grammar, Language, Spelling and Vocabulary

Graphic Design

Health

Housing Decisions

Improving Reading and Study Skills

Indians of Missouri

Introduction to Business

Introduction to Computer Programming: Visual Basic

Introduction to Computers and Information Technology

Introduction to Office Applications

Introduction to Poetry

Introduction to Short Stories

Introduction to Technology

Introductory Agriculture

Introductory Horticulture

Keyboarding/Typewriting

King Arthur and the Middle Ages

Latin 1

Latin 2

Latin 3

continued on next page

**Pennsylvania Cyber
Charter School**
continued from previous page

Marketing/Advertising

Mathematics of Money

Medieval History

MS Office Applications Level 1

Music Appreciation

Mysteries of the Solar System

Mystery Fiction

Mythology

Parenting and Child Development

Pennsylvania Driver's Education

Pennsylvania History

Personal Adjustment, Dating and Marriage

Personal Fitness

Physical Science

Physics

Planning for College

Practical Math

Prealgebra

Precalculus

Project Personal Development

PSSA Mathematics

Psychology

Readings in Science Fiction

SAT Prep, math and verbal

Science Fiction for Reluctant Readers

Search for Identity Through Literature

Social Issues in a Contemporary World

Sociology

Spanish 1

Spanish 2

Spanish 3

Spanish 4

Speak Your Mind: A Guide to Clear Thinking and Communication

Special Topics in Geology

Statistics

The Study of Contemporary Music Trends

Studying Planet Earth: The Satellite Connection

Theater

Trigonometry

The Underground World of Caves

World History

World Religions

Offers diploma? Yes

Tuition: Fi ree

Pinnacle Education Virtual School

2224 W. Southern Ave, Suite 1
Tempe, AZ 85282

Phone: Toll-free (888) 567-1844

Fax: (480) 755-8111

Web site: http://www.pin-ed.com/virtual.asp

E-mail: enrollment@pin-ed.com

Description: On July 14, 2003, Pinnacle Education was authorized by the Arizona State Board for Charter Schools to be a provider of distance learning opportunities for Arizona students. The Pinnacle Virtual High School began serving students in grades 7–12 on August 1, 2003.

Eligibility: Anyone may enroll.

Online high school courses offered:

Algebra 1

American Government

American History

Basic Math

Business Management Technology

Earth Science

English 1

English 2

English 3

English 4

Free Enterprise

Fundamentals of Health

Geometry

Introduction to Art

Life Science

Physical Science

Prealgebra

Sports Marketing

World History

World of Work

Offers diploma? Yes

Tuition: Free to those who attended an Arizona public school during the previous year. Others are charged tuition.

Computer requirements:

Windows-based computers:

Pentium II (233 MHz minimum, higher recommended)

Windows 98, NT, or higher

256 MB RAM

12x CD-ROM (CD/DVD Recommended)

56-K modem

Display setting 800 x 600 resolution (1024 x 768 recommended)

Internet Explorer 5.5 or higher

Flash Player 6

3½" disk drive

Macintosh computers:

Power Mac G3

OS X

3½" disk drive

128 MB RAM

12x CD ROM (CD/DVD Recommended)

56-K modem

Display setting 800 x 600 resolution (1024 x 768 recommended)

Internet Explorer 5.5 or higher

Flash Player 6

Plano ISD eSchool

Plano Independent School District Student Services, PISD eSchool
3540 E. 14th Street
Plano, TX 75074

Phone: (469) 752-8891 or (469) 752-8894

Fax: (469) 752-8885

Web site: http://www.planoisdeschool.net

E-mail: eSchool@pisd.edu

Description: The Plano ISD eSchool will enable students to take high school courses online, on their own time, wherever access is available to the Internet and a computer.

Plano ISD eSchool courses have been developed with the same requirements as traditional high school courses. The courses have been developed to ensure that the curriculum maps to state and national standards. Students have the

continued on next page

Plano ISD eSchool
continued from previous page

opportunity to interact with a group of recognized, experienced, and well-trained teachers as they work through the curriculum independently.

A rich multimedia environment provides engaging, high-quality content for individualized discovery throughout the learning process. Students encounter increasing levels of complexity and sophistication within the course content so that they acquire an ever-widening understanding of the concepts being presented. Courses can be started at any time. Plano ISD eSchool courses are designed to be completed in a minimum of 6 weeks and a maximum of 18 weeks.

Eligibility: Anyone may enroll.

Online high school courses offered:

Algebra 1

Algebra 2

American Government

Business Connections

Career Planning

Chemistry 1

Economics

English 3

English 4

ESL

Geometry 1

Health

Oceanography

Physics 1

Prealgebra

Precalculus

Psychology

Spanish 1

Spanish 2

Study Skills

World Geography

World History

Offers diploma? No

Tuition: $220–$295 per course

Computer requirements:

Windows computer: Pentium Processor and Windows 95 or higher

Macintosh computer: Power PC processor and OS 8.5 or higher

All computers:

64 MB RAM

Color monitor (16-bit, 800 x 600 resolution)

8x or faster CD-ROM drive

Keyboard and mouse

Direct network connection or 56-K modem with Internet access

Sound card and speakers

Hard disk with at least 40 MB available

Microsoft Internet Explorer 5.0 or higher and course-specific plug-ins for the browsers

Microphone for English as a Second Language or Spanish courses

Microsoft Word 97

A printer is recommended

Accreditation: Credits for Plano ISD eSchool are awarded through Plano East Senior High, which is accredited by the Commission on International and Trans-Regional Accreditation, the Commission on Secondary and Middle Schools, and the Southern Association of Colleges and Schools.

Portland State University Independent Study

P.O. Box 1491
Portland, OR 97207-1491

Phone: Toll-free (800) 547-8887 ext. 4865 or (503) 725-4865

Fax: (503) 725-4880

Web site: http://www.istudy.pdx.edu

E-mail: xsis@pdx.edu

Description: Courses offered through Independent Study are correspondence courses, whether you access the materials online or through the printed course guide mailed to your home. In either case, your course will likely require one or more textbooks or other course materials. You can register for and start a course any business day of the year except for university-observed holidays; Independent Study courses do not follow a term schedule. You have 12 months to complete the course work and can purchase a six-month extension if you need more time. You complete the course work anywhere you want to (there are no classroom sessions), turn in assignments on your own schedule, and take exams when you are ready.

Eligibility: Anyone may enroll.

Online high school courses offered:

Algebra I

Biology I and II

Career Education

Corrective English

Current Issues

Earth Science I and II

Freshman English

General Math

General Psychology

General Sociology

Geometry I and II

Global Studies I and II

Government

Junior English

Personal Health I and II

Principles of Economics

Sophomore English

World History I and II

Offers diploma? No. Credits that a student earns are transferred to the student's high school, which awards a diploma

Tuition: $110 per course

Accreditation: Northwest Association of Schools and Colleges

The Potter's School

8279 Raindrop Way
Springfield, VA 22153

Phone: (703) 690-3516

Fax: (703) 690-3516

Web site:
http://www.pottersschool.org

E-mail: director@pottersschool.org

Description: Internet videoconferencing technology has made it possible for students to take live online courses from their homes. Such classes afford home-educated students wonderful opportunities for external instruction in a variety of topics, expanding academic options while supporting home education ideals. The Potter's School provides

continued on next page

The Potter's School

continued from previous page

globally accessible online courses in which the ideals we value as home educators—a biblical worldview, high academic standards, and timely personal feedback—are honored by a dedicated group of teachers who share these values. We offer a full range of core and elective courses for students in grades 7 through 12

Eligibility: Anyone may enroll.

Online high school courses offered:

A.P. Calculus BC

Advanced Algebra

Advanced Chemistry in Creation

Advanced MS Office Applications

Advanced Physics in Creation

Algebra

The American Civil War

American History

Anatomy and Physiology

Ancient History: Along the Nile and Around the Mediterranean

Asia Survey

Aviation Science

Bible Doctrine and Theology

British Literature

Building English Vocabulary From Latin and Greek Roots

Classical Rhetoric I

Classical Rhetoric II

Clear Business Writing

Computer Programming I: Visual Basic.NET

Computer Programming II: C++.NET

Constitutional Law

Days of the Knights: Medieval Times

Early American Literature

Economics

Editing and Proofreading for Business Writers

Elements of Music Theory

English 9th Grade

Exploring Creation With Biology

Exploring Creation With Chemistry

Exploring Creation With Physical Science

Exploring Creation With Physics

Faith and Literature

Fantasy Literature

French I

French II

French III

French IV

French V

From Bach to Bernstein: Classical Music Appreciation From the Middle Ages to the Present

Functions, Statistics, and Trigonometry

Geography

Geometry

German I

German II

God and Government: Advanced Government and Biblical Perspectives

God in All Worlds

Government and the Constitution

Grammar Review and Compositional Writing

Greek and Roman Literature in Translation

History and Culture of the American West

History of the World

HTML With Basic JavaScript

Introduction to Astronomy

Introduction to Business

Introduction to Electronics

Introduction to Literature

A Journey Through Narnia

J. R. R. Tolkien: Lord of the Rings

Junior High French I

Junior High French II

Junior High Latin I

Junior High Latin II

Junior High Spanish I

Koine Greek I

Koine Greek II

Latin I

Latin II

Latin III/IV

Logo to Legos

MS Office Applications

Precalculus and Discrete Mathematics

Propositional Logic

Research Paper Writing

Science Fiction Literature

Shakespeare

Spanish I

Spanish II

Spanish III/IV

Starting Points: Forming Your Biblical Worldview

Survey of Bible History and Culture

Transition Math

Understanding the Times

Western Civilization

Works of C. S. Lewis

World History

World History From a Biblical Perspective

World Literature

The World of Geography

World Religions

Tuition: $210 per semester ($420 per year) for a high school course and $185 per semester ($370 per year) for a junior high course

Computer requirements:

Participation in The Potter's School requires at least a Pentium III 800-MHz PC with 256 MB RAM, a full-duplex audio card, and a microphone (headset with microphone strongly recommended). However, since the Windows XP Service Pack 2 operating system running an antivirus program and firewall consumes approximately 200 MB of RAM memory, we recommend at least 1 GHz processor speed and at least 512 MB RAM memory. Depending on what else is loaded on the PC, some PCs with lower specifications (e.g., 500 MHz and 128 MB RAM) may be able to run the software, but we do not recommend it because performance will be reduced even in the best case. A video camera is optional. A Macintosh, including a Mac emulating a PC, will not run the conferencing software and cannot be used for The Potter's School.

Primavera Online High School

3029 N. Alma School Road, Suite 226-227
Chandler, AZ 85224

Phone: Toll-free (877) 877-4628 or (480) 456-6678

Fax: (480) 820-2168

Web site:
http://www.primaveratech.org

E-mail: info@primaveratech.org

Description: Primavera's curriculum is developed using nationally renowned providers such as Holt Rhinehart and Winston who have made their textbooks available completely online. These online textbooks are innovative and utilize an interactive multimedia-based format that makes learning fun. All Primavera courses are aligned to meet state and national standards, which ensure that your child is getting the highest quality education and preparation for the future.

Course outlines are developed allowing every student to follow a sequential path to complete each class successfully. Students take two courses every six weeks. Each class is structured into 30 two-hour lessons, and is equivalent to half a credit, based upon the Carnegie method for issuing credit. Primavera's innovative course outlines are a simple method that enable students, parents, and faculty to easily follow, understand, and assess each class.

Eligibility: Arizona residents may enroll.

Online high school courses offered:

Advanced Biology Themes

Advanced Composition 12

AIMS Prep

Algebra 1

Algebra 2

American History

American Literature II

American/Arizona Government

Biology 2A Botany/Zoology

Biology 2B Anatomy/Physiology

British Literature 12

Chemistry 1

Composition II

Earth and Space Science

Economics Principles and Practices

Elements of Literature 9

Fundamentals of English 9

Geometry

Health

Learning a Living

Math Fundamentals

Physical Education

Prealgebra

Principles of Biology

Principles of English 10

Spanish 1

Trigonometry

World History

World Literature 10

Offers diploma? Yes

Tuition: Free to Arizona residents

Accreditation: Commission on International and Trans-Regional Accreditation

North Central Association of Colleges and Schools

Providence High School

4101 Tates Creek Center
PMB No.325
Lexington, KY 40517

Phone: Toll-free (866) 4ProvHi
(866-477-6844)

Fax: (859) 499-3434

Web site: http://www.provhigh.com

E-mail: info@provhigh.com

Description: Providence High School
is designed to give students a second
chance to earn a high school diploma.
Our distance education program lets
you study and learn at home. Select
from more than 30 self-paced courses.
You take only the courses you need to
graduate, without disrupting your job,
your family life, or your leisure time.
You will receive textbooks and study
guides in the mail. Study at your own
pace. Take up to a year to complete a
course, or finish early, if you desire.
You set your own pace.

Eligibility: Anyone who has
completed eighth grade or who has
transcripts of high school credits from
another institution

Online high school courses offered:

Algebra I
Algebra II
American Government
Basic Algebra
Basic English
Basic Geometry
Basic Math
Biology
Chemistry
Computer Literacy
Consumer Math
Earth Science
Economics
English Composition
English I
English II
English III
English IV
French I
French II
Geometry
Health/PE
Introduction to General Science
Life Science
Physical Science
Practical English
Prealgebra
Spanish I
Spanish II
Stories to Live By
U.S. Geography
U.S. History
World Geography
World History

Offers diploma? Yes

Tuition: $650 annually or $200 per
course

Computer requirements: Internet
Explorer, e-mail address, printer.

QualitySchoolHouse

2417 Tongass Plaza, Suite 212
Ketchikan, AK 99901

Phone: (907) 225-3274

Fax: (907) 225-3284

Web site:
http://www.qualityschoolhouse.com

E-mail:
registrar@qualityschoolhouse.com

Description: Our classes are taught by
certified teachers and meet criteria
established by Craig City School
District. We utilize Blackboard
Learning Systems, the state-of-the-art
electronic delivery system, and PayPal,
the global leader in online payments,
to ensure your educational satisfaction
and consumer safety. Please browse
our site and get to know us.
QualitySchoolHouse staff are ready to
deliver an exciting learning experience
at your convenience.

Eligibility: Anyone may enroll.

Online high school courses offered:

Algebra

American Government

Biology

Business and Personal Finance

English Literature 9

Environmental Issues in
Oceanography

Geometry

Marine Mammals of Alaska

Oceanography

U.S. History

World Geography

World History

Offers diploma? No

Tuition: $250 per course

Regina Coeli Academy

6429 S. Woodland Hills Drive
Tucson, AZ 85747

Phone: (520) 751-1942

Fax: (520) 751-2580

Web site: http://www.reginacoeli.org

E-mail: admin@reginacoeli.org

Description: Regina Coeli Academy is
the first all-online Catholic
homeschooling program for Roman
Catholics. Our highly qualified faculty
provides academic motivation and
evaluation of home school student
achievement through a liberal arts
program for Catholic homeschooling
families and students in private
schools desiring to supplement their
studies via a classical Catholic
homeschooling program. RCA's
theology program, under Father
Stephen F. Torraco, guides homeschool
students through the Church's
teaching in a four-year sequence,
based on the Universal Catechism of
the Catholic Church.

RCA combines three basic Internet
applications, allowing homeschool
students a complete and excellent
learning experience from their own
homes: live text-based conference
software, a Web browser, and e-mail.
During regularly scheduled live class
meetings, students interact with their
peers and with our highly qualified
faculty. Some courses also offer an
asynchronous enrollment option. This
option assists with home computer
scheduling, as it allows students to
participate in all aspects of the course
(e-mail, automated quizzes, lesson
plans) without the requirement of live
class attendance.

Eligibility: Anyone may enroll.

Online high school courses offered:

Advanced Algebra

Algebra I

American Government

American History

Church History II

Classical English Composition

Confirmation

Cross-curricular English Composition

Geometry

Henle Latin I

Henle Latin II

Henle Latin III

Mastering Composition through Grammar

Material Logic / Rhetoric

Perspectives on Western Civilization I and II

Precalculus

Private Tutoring for Advanced Writers

The Progymnasmata

Theology I

Theology II

Theology III

Theology IV

World Literature

Offers diploma? Yes

Tuition: $360 to $510 per course

Computer requirements:

Windows-based computers:

Pentium or 486 DX (66 MHz minimum; 100 MHz or above recommended)

16 MB RAM recommended

Windows 3.1 or higher

Sound card

Macintosh computers:

OS 7 or higher

8 MB RAM

28.8-K modem or faster

Scholars' Online Academy

6429 S. Woodland Hills Drive
Tucson, AZ 85747

Phone: (520) 751-1942

Fax: (520) 751-2580

Web site:
http://www.islas.org/sola.html

E-mail: admin@islas.org

Description: Scholars' Online Academy is a quality distance learning college preparatory Christian academy that is part of the Institute for Study of the Liberal Arts and Sciences. SOLA brings homeschool students, parents, and teachers together via cutting-edge telecommunications technology. Our four-year liberal arts and science Christian academy provides home education curriculum, which leads to a high school diploma and simultaneously provides diligent homeschool, private school, and public school students an opportunity to complete up to two years of the general education requirements towards a bachelor's degree. All courses are taught from a nonsectarian Christian stance, preparing students to defend the Judeo-Christian tradition not only in the openly hostile university environment but also in what has been called our "post-Christian" world. Our highly qualified

continued on next page

Scholars' Online Academy
continued from previous page

faculty provides stimulation and evaluation of student achievement through four years of English literature and composition, classical languages (either Latin of Greek), science, history, math, government, and philosophy specifically designed for the home education curriculum. RCA combines three basic Internet applications, allowing homeschool students a complete and excellent learning experience from their own homes: live text-based conference software, a Web browser, and e-mail. During regularly scheduled live class meetings, students interact with their peers and with our highly qualified faculty. Some courses also offer an "asynchronous" enrollment option; this option assists with home computer scheduling as it allows students to participate in all aspects of the course (e-mail, automated quizzes, lesson plans) without the requirement of live class attendance.

Eligibility: Anyone may enroll.

Online high school courses offered:

A.P. English

A.P. Latin IV: Virgil

A.P. Latin V: Catullus and Horace

American Literature

Astronomy

Biology

Chemistry

Classical English Composition

Cross-curricular English Composition

English Literature

Greek I

Greek II

Greek III

Greek IV

Greek V

Greek VI

Mastering Composition through Grammar

Medieval Latin

Natural Science I and II

Physics

Private Tutoring for Advanced Writers

The Progymnasmata

Western Literature to Dante

Wheelock Latin I

Wheelock Latin II

Wheelock Latin III

World Literature

Offers diploma? Yes

Tuition: $360 to $510

Computer requirements:

Windows-based computers:

Pentium or 486 DX (66 MHz minimum; 100 MHz or above recommended)

16 MB RAM recommended

Windows 3.1 or higher

28.8-K modem or faster

Sound card

Macintosh computers:

OS 7 or higher

8 MB RAM

28.8-K modem or faster

SeeUonline

P.O. Box 4897
Palmer, AK 99645

Phone: (907) 745-1486

Fax: (907) 745-1442

Web site: http://www.seeuonline.org

E-mail: seeuonline@gaggle.net

Description: Using exciting emerging
technologies as learning tools,
SeeUOnline will provide verbal,
written, and electronic communication
skills to students through online
educational programming tailored to
each registered student. SeeUOnline
can meet the needs of students who
wish to accelerate their learning, are
seeking to complete high school in
less than four years, have scheduling
conflicts or class overloads, or prefer
homeschooling. The program can
accommodate students who have
special medical needs requiring a
home or hospital setting, students
with special needs requiring flexible
programming, and students living in
remote locations or facing commuting
problems.

Eligibility: Anyone may enroll.

Offers diploma? Yes

Tuition: The program is free to
students in the Matanuska-Susitna
Borough School District. Others are
charged tuition.

SK Online

3620 State Street SE
Salem, OR 97301

Phone: (503) 399-3205

Fax: (503) 361-2160

Web site: http://skonline.org

E-mail:
bowman_laura@salkeiz.k12.or.us

Description: SK Online is an
alternative program centrally
delivering Web-based curriculum to
students living in the Salem-Keizer
Public School District as well to
students in Oregon and beyond. Our
purpose is to provide online learning
24 hours a day, seven days a week, to
any school-aged student who needs
acceleration or remediation, is credit
deficient, has scheduling conflicts at
his or her regular school, has medical
considerations, has limited English-
language skills or is homeschooled.

Eligibility: High school students up to
age 21.

Online high school courses offered:

20th Century Studies

Advanced Algebra

Advanced Research and Procedures

Algebra 1

Algebra 1 Theory

Algebra 2

American Government

American History

American Literature

Biology

Business Math

College Writing

continued on next page

SK Online
continued from previous page

Computer Management and Careers

Computer Skills

Concepts in Physical Science

Earth Science

Economics

English 1

English 2

English 9: Composition

English 9: Literature

English Literature

Environmental Chemistry

General Biology

General Math

Geography

Geometry

Global Issues

Health

History in Cinema

Introduction to Advanced Algebra

Introduction to Business

Personal Enhancement

Precalculus

Psychology

Senior Economics

Sophomore Survey 1: Writers' Workshop

Sophomore Survey 2: Literature Survey

Sophomore Economics

Spanish 1

Spanish 4: Literature and Language for Spanish Speakers

Trigonometry

Web Design

Wellness

World History

Offers diploma? Yes, through Roberts High School

Tuition: Students outside Salem-Keizer are charged $120 to $195 per course.

Computer requirements:

PC

Internet Explorer 5.5 or better

Microphone and speaker for some courses

Adobe Acrobat Reader

Accreditation: Northwest Association of Schools and Colleges

South Dakota Virtual Campus

21 Saint Joseph Street
Rapid City, SD 57701

Phone: (605) 394-4028

Web site:
http://www.rcas.org/sdvirtualcampus

E-mail: kimbell.kenner@k12.sd.us

Description: South Dakota Virtual Campus is a school program that will enhance the educational experience of students. It offers students flexibility with scheduling online courses that can be taken anytime at any place where there is access to a computer. Due to the asynchronous nature of the South Dakota Virtual Campus, where students and teachers are not necessarily online at the same time, students can access their online courses anytime to read and participate in assignments, participate in discussions, and submit completed assignments. A master schedule for each course dictates assignments and expectations to help ensure that all participating students are able to be successful in the course. Our half-credit courses run 12 weeks. Full-year courses can be completed in 24 weeks.

Eligibility: Anyone may enroll.

Online high school courses offered:

Algebra 1

Civics

Computer Information Systems

Creative Writing

Current World Affairs

English 9

English 11

Geometry

Information Management Systems

Physiology and Anatomy I and II

Senior Composition

Technical Writing

U.S. Government

U.S. History

Web Page Programming

World Geography

World History

World Literature

Offers diploma? No

Tuition: Students outside the Rapid City school district pay $310 for a semester-long course.

Computer requirements:

A computer (Macintosh or Windows)

An Internet service provider (ISP)

A telephone line to connect to your ISP or a network computer line

Netscape Communicator 7.1 (or higher) or Internet Explorer 5.0 (or higher)

A word processing program, preferably Microsoft Word

Accreditation: North Central Association of Colleges and Schools

Stetson University Virtual School

800 Celebration Avenue
Celebration, FL 34747

Phone: Toll-free (877) 582-0067

Fax: (321) 939-7606

Web site:
http://www.stetson.edu/onlinehighschool

E-mail: jbraden@stetson.edu

Description: The Stetson University Center administers the Florida Virtual School program to out-of-state and international students seeking educational opportunities. We deliver an Internet-based, public high school offering a broad curriculum online, accredited by the Southern Association of Colleges and Schools. Our program has supported the education of thousands of happy students, parents, and educators.

Eligibility: Students from anywhere outside Florida may enroll.

Online high school courses offered:

A.P. Art History

A.P. Biology

A.P. Calculus AB

A.P. Computer Science

A.P. Computer Science AB

continued on next page

Stetson University Virtual School
continued from previous page

A.P. English Language and Composition

A.P. English Literature and Composition

A.P. European History

A.P. Macroeconomics

A.P. Microeconomics

A.P. Spanish Language

A.P. Test Reviews

A.P. U.S. Government and Politics

A.P. U.S. History

Adaptive Personal Fitness IEP or 504 Plan

Algebra I / Algebra I Honors

Algebra II / Algebra II Honors

American Government

American Government Honors

American History / American History Honors

Biology / Biology Honors

Business Sys. Tech

Chemistry / Chemistry Honors

Computer Programming Basic I

Earth Space Science / Earth Space Honors

Economics / Economics Honors

English I / English I Honors

English II / English II Honors

English III / English III Honors

English IV / English IV Honors

Fitness Lifestyle Design

GED Prep

Geometry/Geometry Honors

Global Studies

Latin I

Latin II

Latin III

Liberal Arts Math

Life Management Skills

Marine Science/Marine Science Honors

Personal Fitness

Physics / Physics Honors

Precalculus

SAT Prep

Spanish I

Spanish II

Thinking and Learning Strategies

Web Design I

Web Design II

World History

World History Honors

Offers diploma? Yes

Tuition: $750 for a one-credit course

Computer requirements:

Windows-based computers:

Pentium II (233 MHz minimum, higher recommended)

Windows 98, NT, or higher

256 MB RAM

12x CD-ROM (CD/DVD recommended)

56-K Modem

Display setting 800 x 600 resolution (1024 x 768 recommended)

Printer required

3½" disk drive

Macintosh computers:

Power Mac G3

OS X

3½" disk drive

128 MB RAM

12x CD ROM (CD/DVD Recommended)

56-K Modem

Display setting 800 x 600 resolution (1024 x 768 recommended)

Printer required

Accreditation: Commission on International and Trans-Regional Accreditation

Southern Association of Colleges and Schools

Sycamore Academy

2179 Meyer Place
Costa Mesa, CA 92627

Phone: (714) 668-1343

Fax: (714) 668-1344

Web site:
http://www.sycamoretree.com

E-mail: info@sycamoretree.com

Description: Sycamore Academy offers school online for grades three through twelve. Students do their work on the computer each day and send it to our office through the Internet. All grading and tracking will be done by our teachers. Enrollments are accepted at any time during the school year. Your students will be using the award-winning Switched-On-Schoolhouse curriculum. Curriculum for each subject is on a CD ROM (included in the course fee). Students do the assignments on their own computer and then upload it to our office, where it is checked by credentialed teachers.

The teachers write back to the students. Students may ask any questions and get all the help they need.

Eligibility: Anyone may enroll.

Online high school courses offered:

Algebra 1

Algebra 2

Bible

Biology

Chemistry

College Planner

Consumer Math

Economics

English

Function and Trigonometry

General Science

Geometry

Government

High School Health

Physics

Spanish I

Spanish II

State Histories

The Story of the Constitution

U.S. History

World Geography

World History

Offers diploma? Yes

Tuition: $1200 yearly or $295 per class, plus $100 enrollment fee

Computer requirements:

CD-ROM Multimedia PC

Pentium 133 or better

16 MB RAM

continued on next page

Sycamore Academy
continued from previous page

16-bit sound card capable of 22.05 KHz or better

SVGA video card capable of 640 x 480, 256 colors

4x CD-ROM

Windows 95/98 (not Windows NT)

A printer is recommended

Accreditation: Northwest Association of Academic Schools

Texas Tech University Extended Studies

Texas Tech University
6901 Quaker Avenue
Lubbock, TX 79413

Phone: Toll-free (800) MYCOURSE (800-692-6877)

Fax: (806) 742-7222

Web site: http://www.dce.ttu.edu

E-mail: distlearn@ttu.edu

Description: Texas Tech University offers educational programs to a variety of learners such as K–12 and college students, professionals, and those seeking lifelong learning opportunities. Texas Tech's distance learning programs enable students to pursue educational goals while providing the flexibility needed to maintain professional and personal commitments.

Eligibility: Anyone may enroll.

Online high school courses offered:

Algebra

Biology I

Business Computer Information Systems

Economics: Fundamentals of the Free Enterprise System and Its Benefits

English 9

English 10

English 11

English 12

Foundations of Personal Fitness

Introduction to Business

Personal and Family Development

Sociology

U.S. Government

U.S. History

Web Mastering I

World Geography Studies

Offers diploma? Yes

Tuition: $95 per half credit, plus administrative fees and textbooks/materials

Accreditation: Commission on Colleges of the Southern Association of Colleges and Schools

Texas Virtual School

7145 W. Tidwell Road
Houston, TX 77092-2160

Phone: Toll-free (800) 992-9397

Fax: (713) 744-2775

Web site: http://www.texasvirtualschool.org

E-mail: tcs@esc4.net

Description: The Texas Virtual School is a Web-based learning initiative designed to meet the needs of Texas public school students and educators. Private school students and staff are welcome to take advantage of the programs offered through the Texas Virtual School. Its mission is to provide extended and flexible learning opportunities for secondary students and educators through Web-based programs. Schools can only enroll students for-credit and not-for-credits courses. Educators can enroll in professional development sessions covering an array of topics and roles within the school setting.

Eligibility: Anyone may enroll through their school.

Online high school courses offered:

A.P. Biology

A.P. Calculus AB

A.P. Chemistry

A.P. English Language and Composition

A.P. English Literature and Composition

A.P. Macroeconomics

A.P. Physics A and B

A.P. Psychology

A.P. Spanish

A.P. Statistics

A.P. U.S. Government and Politics

A.P. U.S. History

Algebra I

Basic Computer Information Systems

Biology

Chemistry

English III

Geometry

Health

Practical Writing Skills

Reading

U.S. Government

U.S. History

Offers diploma? No

Tuition: $325 per course ($350 for A.P. courses)

TRECA Digital Academy

1713 Marion-Mt. Gilead Road
Marion, OH 43302

Phone: Toll-free (888) 828-4798 or (740) 725-9158

Fax: (740) 389-6695

Web site: http://tda.treca.org

E-mail: mcarder@treca.org

Description: TRECA Digital Academy (TDA) is an online K–12 public community school working in partnership with local school districts throughout Ohio. TDA offers a unique opportunity to students who have decided that online education is a good alternative to the brick-and-mortar environment.

Students can access their classes 24 hours a day, seven days a week. Students are taught by teachers certified by the State of Ohio Department of Education. Our teachers are in continual communication with students, offering one-on-one feedback and guidance.

Eligibility: Ohio residents may enroll.

Online high school courses offered:

Advanced Math

Algebra I

Algebra II

American History

Art

continued on next page

TRECA Digital Academy
continued from previous page

Astronomy

Biological Science

Chemistry

Child Development

Consumer Math

Creative Writing

Economics

English I

English II

English III

English IV

Environmental Science

Geography

Geometry

German

Health

Integrated Math I

Integrated Math II

Latin

Legends and Leaders

Multimedia I

Music Appreciation

Music Theory

Physical/Earth Science

Physical Education

Psychology

Reading for Pleasure

Spanish

Study Skills

Technology Applications I

U.S. Government

World History

Offers diploma? Yes

Tuition: No

Computer requirements: TDA will provide students all necessary hardware and software

Trent High School

P.O. Box 570
Belmar, NJ 07719

Phone: Not published; prefers e-mail contact

Fax: Not published

Web site: http://www.theschools.com

E-mail: admissions@theschools.com

Description: The mission of the Trent Schools is to provide structured homeschooling lessons that will help students to independently mature as scholars and citizens who are willing to raise questions, weigh evidence, substantiate opinions, and communicate ideas clearly and effectively. Students may begin an individual course at any time. Full-time enrollment begins at the start or midway through the term.

Eligibility: Anyone may enroll.

Online high school courses offered:

Advanced Mathematical Concepts 1 with Trigonometry

Advanced Mathematical Concepts 2 with Trigonometry and Introduction to Calculus

Algebra

Algebra IIA/Statistics

Algebra IIB

Art History 1

Art History 2

Art History 3

Art History 4

Biology

Chemistry 1 Inorganic

Chemistry 2

Early U.S. History

Earth Science

Economics

English 9

English 10

English 11

English 12

French 101

French 201

French 301

French 401

Geometry

German 101

German 201

German 301

German 401

Great American Artists

History/Civics

History of Design

Introduction to Statistics

Modern U.S. History

Natural Science with Health and Hygiene

Physics

Spanish 101

Spanish 201

Spanish 301

Spanish 401

World History

Offers diploma? Yes

Tuition: $672 to $997 for full-time instruction; $75 to $110 for individual courses.

UC College Prep Online

UCCP Headquarters
3004 Mission Street, Suite 200
Santa Cruz, CA 95060

Phone: Toll-free (866) 4UC-PREP (866-482-7737)

Fax: Toll-free (888) FAX4UCC (888-329-4822) or (866) FAXUCCP (866-329-8227) or (831) 460-3070

Web site: http://www.uccp.org

E-mail: uccp@uccp.org

Description: UC College Prep Online provides students the opportunity to advance and enrich their academic experiences through online courses. UCCP provides a core curriculum of online courses that meet the University of California's "a-g" requirements for admission. Students receive most course materials, assignments, and announcements online via the Internet and communicate daily with their instructor. Courses follow a traditional fall, spring, and summer term schedule.

Eligibility: Anyone may enroll.

Online high school courses offered:

A.P. Biology

A.P. Calculus AB

A.P. Calculus BC

A.P. English Language

A.P. Environmental Science

A.P. Macroeconomics

continued on next page

UC College Prep Online
continued from previous page

A.P. Microeconomics

A.P. Physics B

A.P. Physics C

A.P. Spanish Language

A.P. Statistics

A.P. U.S. Government and Politics

A.P. U.S. History

Algebra I

English 9th Grade

English 10th Grade

English 11th Grade

English 12th Grade

Honors Physics

Honors Psychology

Honors Sociology

Introduction to Health

Trigonometry

U.S. Government and Politics

U.S. History

Offers diploma? No

Tuition: $300 to $325 per class

Computer requirements:

Windows-based computers:

400 MHz Pentium II or better (Pentium III or better is recommended)

128 MB RAM

Windows 98 or newer

Monitor with support for 1024 x 768 pixel resolution and 16-bit high color

Sound card and speakers/headphones

CD-ROM drive

Access to a printer and a fax machine, headset, and microphone

Reliable access to the Internet, connection at 56.6 K or better (DSL or better highly recommended)

E-mail account

Microsoft Internet Explorer 5.5 or higher, or Netscape Navigator 6.2 or higher

Macintosh computers:

200-MHz PowerPC or better (G3 or G4 is recommended)

128 MB RAM or more (256 MB for G3, G4, and Mac OS X)

Apple Mac OS 9.1 or newer

Monitor with support for 1024 x 768 pixel resolution and 16-bit high color

Sound card and speakers/headphones

CD-ROM drive

Access to a printer and a fax machine, headset, and microphone.

Reliable access to the Internet, connection at 56.6 K or better (DSL or better highly recommended)

E-mail account

Microsoft Internet Explorer 5.5 or higher, or Netscape Navigator 6.2 or higher

University of Miami Online High School

2585 Glades Circle
Weston, FL 33327

Phone: Toll-free (877) 871-8163 or (305) 689-8647

Web site: http://www.umohs.org

*E-mail:*info@umohs.org

Description: The University of Miami Online High School is a fully accredited private high school that provides students with the flexibility to complete their courses anytime from anywhere in the world. All of their assignments, quizzes, tests, and projects are completed online. Each student has a teacher for each course, with whom he or she communicates by e-mail, instant message, and telephone.

Eligibility: Anyone may enroll.

Online high school courses offered:

A.P. U.S. Government

A.P. Biology

A.P. Calculus

A.P. Chemistry

A.P. English Language and Composition

A.P. English Literature and Composition

A.P. U. S. History

Algebra I

Algebra I Honors

Algebra II

Algebra II Honors

American Government

American Government Honors

American History

American History Honors

Art History

Biology

Biology Honors

Business Systems Technology

Chemistry

Chemistry Honors

Earth/Space Science

Earth/Space Science Honors

Economics

Economics Honors

Emergent Computer Technology

English 1: Survey of Literature

English 2: World Literature

English 3: American Literature

English 4: British Literature

English 1 Honors: Survey of Literature

English 2 Honors: World Literature

English 3 Honors: American Literature

English 4 Honors: British Literature

French I

Geometry

Geometry Honors

Health/Life Management Skills

Marine Science

Online Journalism

Personal Fitness

Physical Education

Physics

Prealgebra

Precalculus

Psychology

SAT Preparatory (English and Math)

Spanish I

Spanish II

Voluntary Community Service

World History

World History Honors

Offers diploma? Yes

Tuition: $9,750 for full time (6 credits) or $1,625 for a one-credit course or $812.50 for a half-credit course

continued on next page

University of Miami Online High School
continued from previous page

Computer requirements:

PC with 500 MHz or higher processor; 233 MHz minimum required; Intel Pentium/Celeron family, AMD family

Windows 2000, XP

Microsoft Office 2000, XP, 2003

128 MB RAM (256 MB–512 MB preferred)

20-GB hard drive or larger

56.6-K-modem, or DSL, or cable modem

Super VGA (800 x 600) or higher resolution video adapter and monitor

Sound card with speakers

CD-ROM (CD-RW recommended for saving large files)

Internet service provider (ISP) account

A current antivirus application (Norton Antivirus preferred)

Microsoft Internet Explorer Version 5.0 or later

Software required for individual classes (check syllabus for each course)

Java 2 Runtime Environment

Flash Player 6

Adobe Acrobat Reader

Accreditation: Commission on International and Trans-Regional Accreditation

Southern Association of Colleges and Schools

University of Missouri – Columbia High School

136 Clark Hall
Columbia, MO 65211-4200

Phone: Toll-free (800) 609-3727 or (573) 882-2491

Fax: (573) 882-6808

Web site: http://cdis.missouri.edu/MUHighSchool/HShome.htm

E-mail: cdis@missouri.edu

Description: The mission of the University of Missouri-Columbia High School is to provide distance learning courses, through a variety of delivery methods, that will complement traditional high school curricula and provide an accredited diploma program for independent learners of all ages seeking an alternative to traditional high school attendance.

MU High School offers a convenient, credible option for homeschool students, rural students seeking college preparation, gifted students seeking challenges, or students who need to catch up on a few courses.

Eligibility: Anyone may enroll.

Online high school courses offered:

A.P. English Literature

Aerospace: Crossing the Space Frontier

Algebra I

Algebra II

American Government

American History Since 1898

American History to 1898

American Literature: Society and Developing Identities

Ancient Egyptian Civilization

Art Appreciation

Biology

Career Explorations

Career Planning: Charting Your Future

Computer Applications

Conservation of Our Natural Resources

Consumer Economics

Creative Writing

Driver Education

English 9th Grade

English 10th Grade

English 11th Grade

English 12th Grade

Environmental Science

Fitness for Well-Being

Foods and Nutrition

General Mathematics

Geometry

Health

Her Stories: Women's Voices in American Literature

Improving Reading and Study Skills

Interactive Spanish I

Introduction to Business

Introduction to Poetry

Music Appreciation

Parenting and Child Development

Physical Science

Physics

Planning for College

Project Personal Development

Readings in the Short Story

Science Fiction for Reluctant Readers

Studying Planet Earth: The Satellite Connection

Teen and Family Living

Trigonometry

The Underground World of Caves

World Geography

World History Since the American Revolution

World History to the American Revolution

World Religions

You and the Law

Offers diploma? Yes

Tuition: $135 per half unit

Accreditation: North Central Association Commission on Accreditation and School Improvement

University of Nebraska – Lincoln Independent Study High School

P.O. Box 888400
Lincoln, NE 68588-8400

Phone: Toll-free (866) 700-ISHS or (402) 472-2175

Fax: (402) 472-1901

Web site: http://nebraskahs.unl.edu

E-mail: extservice@unl.edu

Description: The University of Nebraska-Lincoln Independent Study High School is a fully accredited self-paced curriculum option offering high school courses in a diploma and nondiploma program. Since 1929, Nebraska's High School has been delivering high school courses to students around the world. Nebraska's

continued on next page

University of Nebrasa – Lincoln Independent Study High School
continued from previous page

High School was the first university-based independent study program and is nationally recognized as being a leader in the field. Students may enroll at any time.

Eligibility: Anyone may enroll.

Online high school courses offered:

A.P. U.S. History

Algebra 1st year

Advanced Algebra

Agriscience

American Government: National Level

American Government: Theories, Policies and Politics

American History

American Literature Studies

The American Short Story

Basic Electricity and Electronics

Basic Expository Writing

Basic Grammar

Basic Mathematics

Beginning Accounting

Beginning Piano

Biology

Business and Consumer Mathematics

Business and International Etiquette

Business English and Communication

Business Law

Career Planning

Chemistry With Lab

Chemistry Without Lab

Civics

Consumer Education and Economics

Drawing and Composition

Economics

Effective Methods of Study

Effective Reader Skills

Effective Speech Communication

Elements of Interior Design

English 9th Grade

English 10th Grade

English 11th Grade

English 12th Grade

Ethnic Studies and Human Relations

Family and Personal Etiquette

French 1st year

French 2nd year

French 3rd year

French 4th year

General Homemaking: Clothing and Foods

General Homemaking: Home Management

General Mathematics

General Shop

Geometry

Health Science

Horticulture, Landscaping

Horticulture, Lawn and Plant Care

Intermediate Grammar

Introduction to Black and White Photography

Introduction to Business

Introduction to Driving

Introduction to Human Relations

Introduction to Nutrition

Latin 1st year

Latin 2nd year

Multicultural Literature

Music Theory

Office Systems

Personal Adjustment and Family Living

Personal Finance and Economic Practices

Personal Keyboarding

Physical Science

Physics

Precalculus 1: Analytic Geometry and Algebra

Precalculus 2: Trigonometry

Principles of Art

Psychology

Research: Process and Presentation

Small-Engine Care and Operation

Small-Engine Maintenance and Repair

Sociology

Spanish 1st year

Spanish 2nd year

Spanish 3rd year

Spanish 4th year

World Cultures

World Geography

World History

Offers diploma? Yes

Tuition: The course fee is $130 per course. (Language courses are $250 per course because they are a year long.) Nebraska residents receive a 10% discount on course fees.

Computer requirements:

Netscape 7.0 or higher or Internet Explorer 5.0 or 5.5 or higher

Word processor (i.e., Microsoft Word)

Adobe Acrobat Reader

Minimum Internet connection: 28.8-K modem (56-K modem recommended)

Accreditation: North Central Association Commission on Accreditation and School Improvement

University of Oklahoma High School

1600 Jenkins Avenue, Room 101 Norman, OK 73072-6507

Phone: Toll-free (800) 942-5702 or (405) 325-1921

Fax: (405) 325-7687

Web site: http://ouilhs.ou.edu

E-mail: ouilhs@ou.edu

Description: The University of Oklahoma High School provides the opportunity for teenagers and adults to earn a fully accredited high school diploma through distance learning. Choose from over 100 courses developed and taught by experienced faculty and delivered online or through print. Enhance your academic record with more than 60 freshman and sophomore college courses available for dual high school and college credit.

Eligibility: Anyone may enroll.

Online high school courses offered:

A.P. U.S. Government

Algebra I

Algebra II

American Government

American History

Basic Economics

Beginning Sociology

continued on next page

University of Oklahoma High School
continued from previous page

Biology

English 9th Grade

English 10th Grade

English 11th Grade

English 12th Grade

English 9th Grade Honors

Etiquette: Manners for Today

Excel XP Core

General Mathematics

Geometry

Health and Fitness

Introduction to Astronomy

Introduction to Aviation Science

Introduction to Computers I

Introduction to Computers II

Introduction to Meteorology

Introduction to Psychology

Introduction to the Research Paper

Oklahoma History

Physical Science

Precalculus and Analytic Geometry

Spanish I

Spanish II

Trigonometry

Understanding Art

Word XP Core

World Geography

World History

Offers diploma? Yes

Tuition: High school tuition is $130 per course. Honors and A.P. tuition is $140 per course. Each course carries one half-unit of credit.

Computer requirements: If there is no multimedia (audio, video, Flash exercises, etc.) in a course, then WebCT can be used on a basic 486 DX computer with a dial-up connection and Windows 98. With more advanced technologies such as audio and video, it is recommended to use at least a Pentium III, 1-GHz processor with 512 MB to 1 GB RAM, Windows XP Service Pack 2, and a broadband connection.

Accreditation: Commission on International and Trans-Regional Accreditation

North Central Association Commission on Accreditation and School Improvement

University of Texas at Austin High School

P.O. Box 7700
Austin, TX 78713-7700

Phone: (512) 471-4808

Fax: (512) 475-7933

Web site:
http://www.utexas.edu/cee/dec/uths

E-mail: uths@dec.utexas.edu

Description: Whether you are looking for just one subject or an array of high school subjects, the Distance Education Center can help. Our high school courses offer the flexibility to work at your pace, at your place. Students can take up to nine months to complete a course. Students are required to take the final exam at an approved testing site.

Our new online courses provide a real-world context for learning, multimedia activities that make subjects come alive, and self-assessment tools that help students work to improve their skills. Many of our new courses will not require the purchase of a textbook.

All courses are written by Texas-certified teachers who are experienced in helping students succeed.

Eligibility: Anyone may enroll.

Online high school courses offered:

Algebra 1

Algebra 2

Art 1

Biology 1

Business Computer Information Systems

Chemistry

Communications Applications

Economics

English 1

English 2

English 3

English 4

Food Marketing

Foundations of Personal Fitness

Geometry

Health 1

Individual and Family Life

Integrated Physics and Chemistry

Math Models with Applications

Physical Education 1B: Bowling

Physical Education 1B: Cycling

Physical Education 1B: Golf

Physical Education 1B: Racquetball

Physics

Precalculus

Principles of Marketing

Retailing

Spanish 1

Spanish 2

Spanish 3

U.S. Government

U.S. History

World Geography Studies

World History Studies

Offers diploma? Yes

Tuition: $159 per half credit course

Accreditation: Southern Association of Colleges and Schools

Texas Education Agency

USA International On-Line School

Vilas, CO 81087

Phone: (719) 523-6411

Web site: http://www.usainternationalonlineschool.com

E-mail: bill.hines@vol.vilas.k12.co.us

Description: The USA International Online K–12 School is a premier online kindergarten through 12th grade private school for online students wanting to be homeschooled. This cyber school also has dual credit online college courses for online high school students wanting online college courses. The USA Online School was developed and is operated by the Vilas Interactive Long Distance Alternate School. The USA Online School was designed for the homeschool students who for whatever reason want to be

continued on next page

USA International On-Line School
continued from previous page

homeschooled online. These online students are professional actors, professional athletes, professional rodeo contestants, parents, working students, physically handicapped students, expelled students, students who excel in school, overachievers, and many other students.

Eligibility: Anyone may enroll.

Online high school courses offered:

Algebra I

Algebra I Honors

Algebra II

Algebra II Honors

American Government

American Government Honors

American History

American History Honors

Applied Computer Technology

Biology

Biology Honors

Business Software Applications

Business Systems Technology

Chemistry

Chemistry Honors

Computer Applications

Computer Programming

Earth Space Science

Earth Space Science Honors

English I

English I Honors

English II

English II Honors

English III

English III Honors

English IV

English IV Honors

Fitness Lifestyle Design

Geography

Geometry

Geometry Honors

Global Studies

Latin I

Latin II

Latin III

Life Management Skills

Marine Science

Personal Fitness

Physics

Prealgebra

Precalculus

Spanish I

Web Design I

World History

World History Honors

Offers diploma? Yes

Tuition: $480 per semester per course

Victory Math

1360 Regent Street, Box 151
Madison, WI 53715

Phone: (866) 470-MATH

Web site: http://www.VictoryMath.org

E-mail: Info@TheVictoryMathAcademy.org

Description: Victory Math is a live, online K–12 math program. It guarantees success in improving math performance with its proven anytime, any pace program.

Eligibility: Anyone may enroll.

Online high school courses offered:

Math 7–12: Algebra 1

Math 7–12: Algebra 1 with Saxon

Math 8–12: Geometry

Math 8–12: Integrated 1

Math 9–12: Algebra 2

Math 9–12: Algebra 2 with Saxon

Math 9–12: Consumer Math

Math 10–12: Trigonometry

Math 11–12: Calculus

Offers diploma? Yes

Tuition: $299

Computer requirements:

Pentium III processor

256 KB of RAM

6-GB hard drive

Floppy drive

CD-ROM drive

56-K modem or faster

Windows 98 or higher

We highly suggest a printer.

Accreditation: No

Vilas eSchool

P.O. Box 727
Vilas, CO 81087

Phone: Toll-free (866) 539-4941

Fax: (719) 523-4299

Web site: http://www.vilas.us

E-mail: vilas@vilasonline.org

Description: The Vilas eSchool is providing an education to the youth of Colorado who, for whatever reason, are not being educated by their current public school. We offer a full

and tested K–12 curriculum and also have a wide range of dual credit courses with 13 different Colorado colleges and universities to choose from. With our state-of-the-art delivery system and the comprehensive curriculum, we can offer a first-rate education to any student in the state.

Eligibility: Enrollment in the Vilas eSchool is open to all Colorado students provided they were included in the funded pupil count for a Colorado public school for the previous year.

Online high school courses offered:

Accounting I

Algebra I

Algebra II

American Government

American History

Biology

Biology II

Calculus

Careers

Chemistry

Computer Applications

Consumer Science I

Consumer Science II

English I

English II

English III

English IV

General Business I

General Science

Geography

Geometry

continued on next page

Vilas eSchool
continued from previous page

Internet Literacy

Parenting

PhotoShop

Physical Education

Physics

Prealgebra

Psychology

Spanish I

Spanish II

Trigonometry

Web Building

Work/study Program

World History

Offers diploma? Yes

Tuition: Free

Computer requirements:

Pentium-class computer with a processor speed of 233 MHz or faster

32 MB of RAM

56-K modem

Printer (not absolutely essential but very highly preferred)

CD-ROM drive

Sound card and speakers

Virginia Satellite Educational Network

Virginia Department of Education

P.O. Box 2120

Richmond, VA 23218-2120

Phone: (804) 692-0335

Fax: (804) 225-4514

Web site: http://www.vsenvirginia.org

E-mail: gweisige@pen.k12.va.us

Description: Virginia Satellite Educational Network was designed to provide educational opportunities to small, generally rural schools that have too few students to justify hiring a full-time teacher. It is not uncommon for one or two students per school to enroll in a VSEN course. All courses are broadcast live via satellite and are available for later viewing via VSEN's video archives using the Internet.

Eligibility: Any student may enroll.

Online high school courses offered:

A.P. Calculus

A.P. English

A.P. Government

A.P. Statistics

A.P. U.S. History

Japanese I

Japanese II

Japanese III

Latin I

Latin II

Latin III

Offers diploma? No

Tuition: Virginia residents are not charged tuition. Others are charged $375 per course.

Virtual Advanced Placement School

Virginia Department of Education
P.O. Box 2120
Richmond, VA 23218-2120

Phone: Toll-free (800) 246-8736

Fax: (804) 225-4514

Web site:
http://www.pen.k12.va.us/VDOE/Technology/VAPScourses.html

E-mail: cathy.cheely@doe.virginia.gov

Description: The Virtual Advanced Placement School provides a variety of college-level and foreign language courses, using distance learning technologies. The school was designed to provide educational opportunities to schools that may have too few students to justify hiring a full-time teacher or are unable to find qualified teachers, and for students with scheduling conflicts. Advanced placement courses follow the College Board curriculum. Foreign language courses are open to students from the seventh grade and higher.

Eligibility: The school is open to all Virginia public school students. Out-of-state and private school students should contact individual course providers to determine seat availability in online courses.

Online high school courses offered:

A.P. Biology

A.P. Chemistry

A.P. English Language/Composition

A.P. English Literature

A.P. European History

A.P. Human Geography

A.P. Macroeconomics

A.P. Microeconomics

A.P. Physics B

A.P. Psychology

A.P. Spanish Language

A.P. U.S. Government and Politics

A.P. U.S. History

Offers diploma? No

Tuition: $375 to $600 per course for out-of-state and online courses. There is no fee for Virginia public school students participating in the Early College Scholars program.

Virtual Community School of Ohio

6100 Channingway Boulevard, Suite 202
Columbus, OH 43232

Phone: Toll-free (866) 501-9473 or (614) 501-9473

Fax: (614) 501-9470

Web site: http://www.vcslearn.org

E-mail: info@vcslearn.org

Description: Virtual Community School of Ohio offers a statewide, comprehensive educational program for Ohio students in grades K–12.

Eligibility: Ohio residents may enroll.

Online high school courses offered:

Advanced Math

Algebra I

Algebra II

American History

Art 1

Art History

continued on next page

Virtual Community School of Ohio
continued from previous page

Basic Computer Skills

Basic Reading Skills

Basic Study Skills

Basic Writing Skills

Biology

Business Math

Chemistry

Classical Tragedies

Drama

Earth Science

French I

French II

Geometry

Health

Introduction to Algebra

Language Arts I

Language Arts II

Language Arts III

Language Arts IV

Life Science

Life Skills

Math 1

Math 2

Multi Media Technology

Office XP

Physical Education

Physical Science

Physics

Psychology

Spanish I

Spanish II

Spanish III (Independent Study)

Title 1 Reading and Writing

U.S. Government

World History

Offers diploma? Yes

Tuition: Free

Virtual Greenbush

P.O. Box 189

947 W. 47 Highway

Girard, KS 66743

Phone: (620) 724-6281

Web site:
http://www.virtualgreenbush.org

E-mail: vgbinfo@greenbush.org

Description: Virtual Greenbush courses are unique from other Web-based courses because of their interactivity and student-centered focus. All the tools and materials a student needs to take a course are contained within the course, with a few exceptions where a textbook may be needed.

Students are responsible for their own learning with guidance from the teacher. Students make choices in the paths they take and select from many different learning activities and experiences. Students encounter increasing levels of complexity and sophistication within the course content so that they acquire an ever-widening understanding of the concepts being presented.

Eligibility: Anyone may enroll through their local school.

Online high school courses offered:

A.P. English Language

A.P. English Literature

Advanced Composition

Advanced Creative Writing

Advanced Music Theory

Algebra 1

Algebra 2

American Government

American History 1

American Literature 1

Anthropology

Archeology: Digging into the Past

Art History

Basic Music Theory

Beginning Composition

Biology 1

Business and Consumer Math

Business and Personal Protocol

Business Communication

Career Planning

Chemistry 1

Civics

Computer Programming Basic II

Conversational English: Everyday English

Conversational English: Explore Your World

Creative Writing

Driver's Education

English 9

English 10

English 11

English 12

French 1

French 2

Geometry 1

German 1

German 2

Health Sciences 1

International Business

Introduction to Technology

Kansas History

Life Management Skills

Macroeconomics

Man vs. Nature in Literature

Math Skills Review

Music Appreciation

Music Composition

Music History

Oceanography

Personal Economics and Finance

Physics 1

Prealgebra 1

Precalculus 1a: Analytic Geometry

Precalculus 1b: Trigonometry

Psychology

Reading Comprehension

Science Fiction In Literature and Film

Spanish 1

Spanish 2

Study Skills: Learning Fundamentals

SuperStructures

Utopia/Dystopia in Literature

Web Design

World Civilizations 1

World Literature

Offers diploma? Yes

Tuition: Most semester-long courses cost $295, and most year-long courses cost $590.

Computer requirements:

Pentium running at least Windows 98 or Mac with OS 9 or greater

continued on next page

Virtual Greenbush
continued from previous page

Direct network access or 56-K modem with Internet access

8x or greater CD-ROM

64 MB RAM

Hard drive with 40 MB space available

Color monitor (16-bit, 800 x 600 resolution minimum)

Sound card and speakers

Keyboard and mouse

Internet Explorer 5.0 or higher (only supported browser)

Course-specific plug-ins included on the CD

Microphone for Conversational English or some foreign language courses

Accreditation: Commission on International and Trans-Regional Accreditation

North Central Association Commission on Accreditation and School Improvement

Virtual High School

2 Clock Tower Place, Suite 500
Maynard, MA 01754

Phone: (978) 897-1900

Fax: (978) 897-9839

Web site: http://www.govhs.org

Description: Imagine classrooms without walls, where students are able to attend their classes 24 hours a day, seven days a week. Imagine students working cooperatively online with others from a wide variety of ethnicities, backgrounds, and geographic locations. What you are beginning to imagine is the reality of the Virtual High School, a nonprofit organization that offers content-rich, credit-bearing high school courses to students across the country and around the world.

Although the student has the flexibility to access his or her class any time 24 hours a day, seven days a week, there are definite due dates and scheduled deadlines for assignments and activities.

Eligibility: Anyone may enroll.

Online high school courses offered:

101 Ways to Write a Short Story Section

Pre-A.P. Biology

Pre-A.P. Calculus

Pre-A.P. Chemistry

Pre-A.P. Computer Science

Pre-A.P. Economics

Pre-A.P. English Language and Composition

Pre-A.P. English Literature and Composition

Pre-A.P. Environmental Science

Pre-A.P. Government

Pre-A.P. Physics B

Pre-A.P. Statistics

Pre-A.P. U.S. History

A.P. Biology

A.P. Calculus AB

A.P. Calculus BC

A.P. Chemistry

A.P. Computer Science A

A.P. Economics: Micro and Macro

A.P. English Language and Composition

A.P. Environmental Science: A Passage to Know, to Love, and Then to Keep the Earth

A.P. French Language

A.P. Physics B

A.P. Physics C

A.P. Spanish Language/Spanish V

A.P. Statistics

A.P. U.S. History

Academic Writing Section

Algebra 1

Algebra 2

American Foreign Policy

American Popular Music

Anatomy and Physiology: A Study in Stability

Animal Behavior and Zoology

Animation and Effects

Astronomy: Stars and the Cosmos

Basic Chemistry

Bioethics Symposium

Biotechnology

Business and Personal Law

Calculus for Business

Career Awareness for the New Millennium

Caribbean Art History

Chemistry II: Chemicals of Civilization

Computational Science and Engineering Using Java

Constitutional Law

Contemporary American Poetry

Contemporary Irish Literature

Creating Art History

Creative Writing for People Who Mean It: Advanced Imaginative Writing

Cultural Identity Through Literature: Understanding Place

Democracy in America?

Desktop Publishing: In an Information Age

Digital Geography: More Than a Jeopardy Category!

DNA Technology

Eastern and Western Thought

Employability Skills

Engineering Principles

English 9

English 10

English Literary Foundations

Entrepreneurs: Business Owners of the 3rd Millennium

Entrepreneurship: Starting Your Own Business

Environmental Chemistry

Environmental Science: The World Around Us

Evolution and the Nature of Science

Exploring Biology

Exploring Chemistry

Exploring Computer Science

Exploring Economics

Exploring English Literature

Exploring Environmental Science

Exploring Physics

Exploring Psychology

Exploring Statistics

Exploring U.S. History

Folklore and Literature of Myth, Magic, and Ritual

continued on next page

Virtual High School
continued from previous page

Fractals: What Are They? What Are They Used For?

Gateway Math

Gateway Reading and Literary Analysis

Gateway Writing

Genes and Disease: The Inheritance of Human Genetic Disorders

Ghoulies, Ghosties, and Long-Legged Beasties: Why We Like to be Scared

Gods of CNN: The Power of Modern Media

The Golden Age of Classical Greece

Great Inventions and Scientific Discoveries

Health

Hearts of Darkness: Meeting Ourselves in Literature

Heroes

History and Pop Music: 20th Century History and American Pop Music

History of Photography

The Holocaust

Horror, Mystery and Science Fiction Literature: Edgar Allen Poe to the Present

IB Economics

Integrated Mechanical Physics with Logical Reasoning: Mechanics in Physics

International Business: An Exploration

Introduction to Astronomy: Stars and the Cosmos

Introduction to Programming in Visual Basic

Introduction to Sociology

Investing in the Stock Market

Learning to Invest in the Stock Market

Lewis and Clark's Expedition: An Interactive Journey

Marketing and the Internet

Math You Can Use In College

Mathematical Reasoning and Logic

Meteorology: A Study of Atmospheric Interactions

Music Composition and Arranging

Music Listening and Critique

Mythology: Stories from Around the World, From the Beginning of Time, to the End of the Earth

Nuclear Physics: Science, Technology and Society

Number Theory: Patterns, Puzzles and Cryptography

Parenting in the Twenty-First Century

Peacemaking

Pearl Harbor to the Atomic Bomb: The Pacific War, 1941–1945

Personal Finance

Perspectives in Health

Poetry Writing

Practical Law: What You Need to Know About the Law

Preveterinary Medicine

Psychology: An Introduction

Reading and Writing the Science Fiction Short Story

Screenwriting Fundamentals

Service-Learning

Sports and American Society

Statistics and Business Quality Management

Technology and Multimedia

To Kill a Mockingbird: Maycomb—Microcosm to the World

Twentieth Century Women Authors: A Reflection of a Changing America

U.S. History

The Vietnam War

Web Design and Internet Research

Web Design: Artistry and Functionality

Western Cultural Humanities: A Tour of Arts and Ideas

World Area Studies: Ancient and Modern Civilizations

World Conflict, a United Nations Introduction

Writing and Telecommunications: Write On For Real

Writing in Spanish

Young Adult Literature: Issues in Tolerance and Diversity

Offers diploma? No

Tuition: Varies

Virtual High School@PWCS

1500 Graduation Drive
Haymarket, VA 20169

Phone: (571) 261–4517

Fax: (571) 261-4411

Web site:
http://www.pwcs.edu/pwcsvirtualhs

E-mail: jonesgk@pwcs.edu

Description: The Office of Instructional Technology for Prince William County Schools provides an alternative educational opportunity for students through the Virtual High School. We have designed and developed online courses that students may take for high school credit.

Eligibility: These courses are open to all students enrolled in an accredited base high school.

Online high school courses offered:

A.P. Biology

A.P. Government

Algebra I

Algebra II

Astronomy

Biology I

Chemistry

Classroom Driver Education

Computer Graphic Design

Creative Writing

Earth Science

English 9

English 10

English 11

English 12

Geometry

Health

Physical Education

Spanish III

U.S. and Virginia Government

U.S. and Virginia History

World Geography

World History (1500–present)

Offers diploma? No

Tuition: $425 for a student in the PWC district; $570 for others

Computer requirements:

Pentium processor with Windows 98 or better

Microsoft Word and PowerPoint 98 or better

continued on next page

Virtual High School at PWCS
continued from previous page

Hard drive with at least 1 GB available

64 MB RAM

Color monitor (16-bit)

8x or faster CD-ROM

Keyboard, mouse, sound card, and speakers

Direct network connection or 56-K modem with Internet access

Netscape Communicator 4.61 or Microsoft Explorer 5.0

Additional plug-ins and updates may be required with certain courses

Warren County Virtual Community School

320 E. Silver Street
Lebanon, OH 45036

Phone: (513) 695-2567 or
(513) 695-2911

Fax: (513) 695-2961

Web site: http://wcvcs.com

E-mail: wb_wcvcs@swoca.net

Description: Warren County Virtual Community School's mission is to provide students with a highly personal and continuous connection to learning through an Internet-based education. We believe that people are empowered by their independent use of information technologies and that they are united by opportunities to share resources and communicate in our local and global communities. We deem that this quality instructional alternative will serve individual needs and prepare the student to be a contributing member of society. The WCVCS will develop in each student the art of communication, the ability to engage in critical thinking, and to demonstrate the mastery of the academic building blocks necessary for a successful future.

Eligibility: Limited to students living within 50 miles of Lebanon, Ohio.

Online high school courses offered:

Algebra 1

Algebra 2

Art History

Biology

Biology with Lab

British Literature

Creative Writing

Drama in Literature

Earth Science

Economics

English Fundamentals

English Internet Explorations

French 1 and 2

General Science

Geometry

Health

History of America

History of the World

Honors American History

Honors American Literature

Honors Biology with Lab

Honors Biology

Honors Drama Literature

Honors Earth Science

Honors English Fundamentals

Honors Oceanography

Honors Physics (includes Lab)

Honors Shakespearean Literature

Honors World History

Honors World Literature

Introduction to the Internet

Journal Writing

Life Management

Literature of America

Literature of the World

Math Proficiency

Mythology

Oceanography

Photoshop Design

Physics with Lab

Prealgebra

Renaissance Art

SAT Prep

Shakespearean Literature

Spanish 1

Spanish 2

Spanish 3

Special Needs: Integrated Science

Study of the Environment

Survival Math

U.S. Government

World Cultures

Writing Tutorials

Offers diploma? Yes

Tuition: None

Computer requirements: The student will be provided with an appropriate computer.

Accreditation: Ohio Department of Education

West Virginia Virtual School

West Virginia Department of Education
1900 Kanawha Boulevard E.
Charleston, WV 25305

Phone: (304) 558-7880

Web site:
http://virtualschool.k12.wv.us

E-mail: phoppe@access.k12.wv.us

Description: The West Virginia Department of Education approves courses to be offered via the West Virginia Virtual School from distance learning companies, organizations, and K–12 and higher education institutions. These companies, organizations, and institutions are the content providers. A student will take courses directly from these providers once the approval process is completed.

Eligibility: Must be a resident of West Virginia. Register through local school.

Online high school courses offered:

A.P. Art History

A.P. Biology

A.P. Calculus AB

A.P. Calculus

A.P. Chemistry

A.P. Computer Science A

A.P. Computer Science AB

A.P. English Language (Honors)

A.P. English Language and Composition

A.P. English Literature and Composition

A.P. French Language

continued on next page

West Virginia Virtual School
continued from previous page

A.P. Macroeconomics

A.P. Microeconomics

A.P. Physics B

A.P. Physics C: Electricity and Magnetism

A.P. Physics C: Mechanics

A.P. Psychology

A.P. Spanish Language

A.P. Statistics

A.P. U. S. Government and Politics

A.P. U.S. History

Advanced Composition

African American Literature

American Government

American Government

American History

American Literature

Astronomy (Honors)

Basic Geometry: Geometry in Our World

Beginning Composition: A Writing Road Trip

British Literature

Business Systems Technology

C++

Calculus A

Calculus B

Calculus C

Career Planning

Chemistry

Children's Literature (Honors)

Civics

Communication Skills

Computer Applications

Computer Programming Basic 1

Economics

Elementary Essay Writing

English 1

English 2

English 3

English 4

English as a Second Language

English Language and Composition

Expository Writing

Fiction Literature

French 1

French 2

French 3

French 4 (Honors)

Geography

Geometry

German 1

German 2

German 3

German 4 (Honors)

Global Studies

Health 1

History of Asia (Honors)

History of the Crusades (Honors)

History of the Holocaust (Honors)

Honors Geometry

Intermediate Essay Writing

Introduction to Design

Introduction to Floriculture (Honors/FFA)

Introduction to HTML

Introduction to Internet

Introduction to Java

Introduction to Music Theory

Introduction to Paralegal Studies (Honors)

Introduction to Photography

Introduction to Sign Language 1

Japanese 1

Japanese 2

Language Arts 9

Language Arts 10

Language Arts 11

Latin 1

Latin 2

Latin 3

Macroeconomics

Marine Science

Medical Assisting (Honors)

Mexican American Literature

Music Theory

Native American History (Honors)

Native American Literature

Oceanography

Oceanography (Honors)

Personal Economics and Finance

Physics 1

Political Science (Government)

Practical Math

Practical Writing

Precalculus

Programming in C

Psychology

Reading Comprehension

SAT Prep/Critical Thinking Skills

Science Fiction Literature (Honors)

Sociology (Honors)

Spanish 1

Spanish 2

Spanish 3

Spanish 4 (Honors)

Study Skills

Theatre Arts (Honors)

Trigonometry (Honors)

Web Design 1

Word Processing 2

World History

World Literature

World Mythology (Honors)

Offers diploma? No

Tuition: $200 to $450. Local school districts may pay tuition through instructional budgets. Parents may be requested to pay tuition if the course is offered at the school and there is no justifiable need to duplicate the course offering.

Westside Virtual High School

3534 S. 108th Street
Westside CCC
Omaha, NE 68144

Phone: (402) 390-8335

Fax: (402) 390-8325

Web site: http://wvhs.westside66.org

E-mail: cdefrey@westside66.org

Description: Westside Virtual High School provides students with online high school courses by utilizing the unique capabilities and qualities of the World Wide Web. These online courses have been created by Class.com, a privately held company founded in 1998 and headquartered in Lincoln, Nebraska, that works with

continued on next page

Westside Virtual High School
continued from previous page

education agencies and local school districts to establish virtual schools using Internet-based content.

Eligibility: Anyone may enroll.

Online high school courses offered:

Advanced Composition

Algebra 1

Algebra 2

American Government

American History 1

American Literature 1

Anthropology

Beginning Composition

Biology 1

Business and Consumer Math

Business and Personal Protocol

Business Communication

Career Planning

Chemistry 1

Civics

Conversational English: Everyday English

Conversational English: Explore Your World

Geometry 1

Health Science 1

Introduction to Technology

Life Science: Oceanography

Macroeconomics

Math Skills Review

Personal Economics and Finance

Physics 1

Prealgebra 1

Precalculus 1

Psychology

Reading Comprehension

Spanish 1

Spanish 2

Study Skills

World Civilizations 1

World Literature

Offers diploma? No

Tuition: $300 per course

Computer requirements:

Mac OS 8.5 or higher, or Pentium or other recent processor

64 MB RAM

Color monitor (16-bit, 800 x 600 resolution)

8x or faster CD-ROM

Keyboard and mouse

Internet access

56-K modem minimum (cable modem or DSL suggested)

Hard drive with at least 40 MB available

Netscape Communicator 4.74 or Microsoft Internet Explorer 5 with plug-ins Microphone for a language-based course

Sound card and speakers

Accreditation: North Central Association of Colleges and Schools

State of Nebraska

Wichita eSchool

412 S. Main Street
Wichita, KS 67202

Phone: (316) 973-5181

Fax: (316) 973-7916

Web site: http://eschool.usd259.org

E-mail: smorris@usd259.net

Description: Wichita eSchool online courses are available to students across the nation who need an alternative way to earn course credits toward a diploma. Students may need to recover course credit for failed classes, or students may need to take a course online because they have a full course load and can't fit everything into a regular school day. Another reason for having students take an online class relates to nationwide budget cuts in education funding. Sometimes with these cuts schools can't offer their students courses that are needed for college or for enrichment. The facilitator at a student's attending high school will receive semester finals through e-mail and will monitor face-to-face finals to verify that the enrolled student is the person who takes the final.

Eligibility: Anyone may enroll.

Online high school courses offered:

A.P. Calculus

Algebra 1

Algebra 2

Biology

Chemistry

Computer Applications 1

Computer Applications 2

Computer Presentation

Earth Space Science

English 1

English 2

English 3

English Composition

English Composition: College Reading

Geometry

Government

Informal Geometry

Introduction to Art

Keyboarding

Music Appreciation

Physical Science Survey

Prealgebra

Precalculus

Sociology

Spanish 1

Trigonometry

U.S. History 1

U.S. History 2

World History

World Literature

Offers diploma? No. Credits and grades are sent to student's school.

Tuition: $150 per half-credit, semester course

Computer requirements:

PC computer with speakers and sound card

Internet connection and Web browser, preferably Netscape 4.0 or higher or Internet Explorer 6.0 or higher

E-mail account

Microsoft Word

Accreditation: Kansas Department of Education

York County School Division Virtual High School

York County School Division
302 Dare Road
Yorktown, VA 23692

Phone: (757) 898-0454

Fax: (757) 890-0771

Web site:
http://yorkcountyschools.org/
VirtualHS

E-mail: rfox@ycsd.york.va.us

Description: The York County School Division Virtual High School provides a comprehensive online program that offers a full suite of academic and elective courses. The courses are interactive and engaging with a wide range of activities, assignments, research, and discussion.

Eligibility: Anyone may enroll.

Online high school courses offered:

A.P. Chemistry (through Virtual Advanced Placement School)

A.P. English 12

A.P. European History (through Virtual Advanced Placement School)

Algebra I

Algebra II

Art Heritage

Biology I

Business Finance

Business Law

Business Management

Chemistry I

Computer Repair I

Computer Repair II

Computer Systems Technology I

Computer Systems Technology II

Earth Science

Ecology and Environmental Science

English 9

English 10

English 11

English 12

Geometry

Health and PE 9

Health and PE 10

Life Planning

Math Algebra Concepts

Mathematical Analysis

Personal Finance

Physics I

Practical Math

Psychology

Sociology

Spanish I

Spanish II

Spanish III

Survey of World Drama

Virginia and U.S. Government

Virginia and U.S. History

Web Design I

Web Design II

World Geography

World History I

World History II

Offers diploma? No

Tuition: $525 per course

Computer requirements:
Windows-based computers:

Windows 95, 98, 2000, XP, or NT

At least 233-MHz processor

32 MB of RAM

Super VGA monitor or higher resolution monitor

Active Internet connection

CD-ROM drive

Sound card and speakers

Macintosh computers:

PowerPC-based Mac running at 100 MHz or higher

OS 7.5.3 or later version

24 MB RAM with virtual memory turned on

Macintosh-compatible monitor or higher resolution monitor

Active Internet connection

CD-ROM drive

Sound card and speakers

Course
Index

F ollowing is an index of all the online courses offered by the institutions profiled in this book—more than 4,500 in all. The courses are grouped under disciplines such as History and Mathematics. Advanced Placement (A.P.) courses are listed with other courses in the same discipline, not under a separate "Advanced Placement" heading.

Even if an institution uses Roman numerals in its course titles (e.g., Algebra I), this index uses only Arabic numerals (e.g., Algebra 1), for ease of comparison across high schools. A variety of miscellaneous courses is listed at the end of the index.

Please note: A course title is only a rough guide to what a course will cover. Often, online courses at two institutions with the same title may be very similar, or even identical, if they both obtain the course from the same company. On the other hand, courses at different institutions with the same title may have very different content. Or similar courses may have different titles at different institutions. Before you register for a course, check with the institution to make sure that it will fit your needs.

Arts and Music

20th Century Music
The Grace Academy
The Jubilee Academy
The MorningStar Academy

A.P. Art History
Florida Virtual School
Intelligent Education
iQ Academies
Kentucky Virtual High School
Maryland Virtual Learning
    Opportunities
Michigan Virtual High School
Monroe Virtual High School
Stetson University Virtual School
West Virginia Virtual School

A.P. Music Theory
Intelligent Education

Advanced Digital Photography
National University Virtual High
    School

Advanced Music Theory
Futures International High School
Virtual Greenbush

American Film Survey
Michigan Virtual High School
American Popular Music
Virtual High School

Architecture
Eldorado Academy

Art
American Virtual High School
Colorado State Academy
Elkhart Cyber School
TRECA Digital Academy

Art 1
Choice 2000 Online High School
Clintondale Virtual High School
Monroe Virtual High School
University of Texas at Austin High
    School
Virtual Community School of Ohio

Art and Music 9–12: Continuing Your Exploration
The Grace Academy
The Jubilee Academy
The MorningStar Academy

Art and Music Appreciation
Babbage Net School
Keystone National High School

Art Appreciation
Cumberland County Schools' Web
    Academy
E-School
Futures International High School
Monroe Virtual High School
PA LEARNERS Online Regional
    Cyber Charter School
Pennsylvania Cyber Charter School
University of Missouri-Columbia
    High School

Art Exploration
PA LEARNERS Online Regional
    Cyber Charter School

Art Foundations
Electronic High School

Art Heritage
York County School Division Virtual
    High School

Art History
3D Learn
CompuHigh/Whitmore School
James Madison High School Online
Laurel Springs School
Michigan Virtual High School
Oregon Online
Pennsylvania Cyber Charter School
University of Miami Online High
    School
Virtual Community School of Ohio
Virtual Greenbush
Virtual High School
Warren County Virtual Community
    School

Fine Arts Survey
  Louisiana Virtual School
From Bach to Bernstein: Classical Music Appreciation from the Middle Ages to the Present
  The Potter's School
Fundamentals of Engineering Drawing
  Intelligent Education
Fundamentals of Music
  North Dakota Division of
    Independent Study
Fundamentals of Music Theory
  Education Program for Gifted Youth
Graphic Design
  iQ Academies
  Pennsylvania Cyber Charter School
Great American Artists
  Trent High School
History and Pop Music
  Virtual High School
History in Cinema
  SK Online
The History of Ancient Art
  Blueprint Education
History of Christian Music
  The Grace Academy
  The Jubilee Academy
  The MorningStar Academy
History of Design
  Trent High School
History of Photography
  Virtual High School
Integrated Drawing
  Oak Meadow School
Interior Design
  Electronic High School
Interior Design and Housing
  Cumberland County Schools' Web
    Academy
Intermediate Drawing and Painting
  Blueprint Education

Intermediate Piano
  Monroe Virtual High School
Introduction to Art
  Basehor-Linwood Virtual School
  OSU K–12 Online
  Pinnacle Education Virtual School
  Wichita eSchool
Introduction to Black and White Photography
  Monroe Virtual High School
  University of Nebraska-Lincoln
    Independent Study High School
Introduction to Design
  Intelligent Education
  West Virginia Virtual School
Introduction to Design Honors
  Intelligent Education
Introduction to Digital Photography
  National University Virtual High
    School
Introduction to Drawing
  Intelligent Education
Introduction to Music
  K–12 Distance Learning Academy
Introduction to Music Theory
  West Virginia Virtual School
Introduction to Photography
  Intelligent Education
  West Virginia Virtual School
Introduction to Theatre
  Illinois Virtual High School
Introductory Photography
  Monroe Virtual High School
Knowing About Art
  North Dakota Division of
    Independent Study
Mechanical Drawing
  Intelligent Education
Media Literacy – Fine Arts
  Laurel Springs School
Movie Review
  On Line Academy

Business

Accounting
Blueprint Education
Colorado Online Learning
Colorado State Academy
Eagle Christian School
Eldorado Academy
Monroe Virtual High School
NorthStar Academy
Pennsylvania Cyber Charter School

Accounting 1
Maryland Virtual Learning
Opportunities
Vilas eSchool

Advertising and Promotion
Electronic High School

Basic Accounting 1
Intelligent Education

Basic Accounting 2
Intelligent Education

Beginning Accounting
Monroe Virtual High School
University of Nebraska-Lincoln
Independent Study High School

Bookkeeping
Oak Meadow School

Business and Financial Management 1
Cumberland County Schools' Web
Academy

Business and Financial Management 2
Cumberland County Schools' Web
Academy

Business and International Etiquette
Monroe Virtual High School
University of Nebraska-Lincoln
Independent Study High School
Business and Personal Protocol
Illinois Virtual High School
Karval Online Education

Minnesota Center of Online Learning
Westside Virtual High School

Business Communication
Electronic High School
Illinois Virtual High School
Karval Online Education
Michigan Virtual High School
Minnesota Center of Online Learning
Monroe Virtual High School
Virtual Greenbush
Westside Virtual High School

Business Computer Information Systems
Houston Independent School District
Virtual School

Business Connections
Plano ISD eSchool

Business English and Communication
Monroe Virtual High School

Business Finance
York County School Division Virtual
High School

Business Management
Intelligent Education
York County School Division Virtual
High School

Business Management Technology
Pinnacle Education Virtual School

Business Systems Technology
Florida Virtual School
James Madison High School Online
Monroe Virtual High School
Stetson University Virtual School
University of Miami Online High
School
USA International On-Line School
West Virginia Virtual School

Business Technology
Alabama Online High School

Career Tech Coordinated Studies
PA LEARNERS Online Regional
Cyber Charter School

Office Systems
 Monroe Virtual High School
 Monroe Virtual High School
Principles of Marketing
 University of Nebraska-Lincoln
  Independent Study High School
 University of Texas at Austin High
  School
Retailing
 University of Texas at Austin High
  School
Salesmanship
 Blueprint Education
Small Business/Entrepreneurship
 Cumberland County Schools' Web
  Academy
**Sports and Entertainment
Marketing**
 Electronic High School
Sports Marketing
 Pinnacle Education Virtual School
Sports/Entertainment Marketing
 Northern Star Online
**Statistics and Business Quality
Management**
 Virtual High School

Computers

3D Animation 1
 Keystone National High School
3D Animation 2
 Keystone National High School
3D Programming 1
 3D Learn
A.P. Computer Programming (JAVA)
 Gwinnett County Online Campus
A.P. Computer Science
 E-School
 Kentucky Virtual High School
 Michigan Virtual High School
 NorthStar Academy

A.P. Computer Science A
 Center for Talent Development
 Florida Virtual School
 Intelligent Education
 Maryland Virtual Learning
  Opportunities
 New Jersey Virtual School
 Stetson University Virtual School
 Virtual High School
 West Virginia Virtual School
A.P. Computer Science AB
 Florida Virtual School
 Intelligent Education
 Stetson University Virtual School
 West Virginia Virtual School
Advanced MS Office Applications
 The Potter's School
Advanced Web Design
 Northern Star Online
Advanced Web Page Design
 Gwinnett County Online Campus
Animation and Effects
 Virtual High School
Applied Computer Technology
 USA International On-Line School
Assembly Language Programming
 Illinois Virtual High School
**Basic Computer Information
Systems**
 Texas Virtual School
Basic Computer Skills
 Virtual Community School of Ohio
Basic Keyboard
 Central Connecticut Adventist
  Virtual School
Basic Microsoft Office Skills
 Pennsylvania Cyber Charter School
Beginning HTML
 Eagle Christian School
Business Computer Applications
 Elkhart Cyber School

Computer Programming
USA International On-Line School
Computer Programming 1: Visual Basic .NET
The Potter's School
Computer Programming 2: C++ .NET
The Potter's School
Computer Programming Basic
Monroe Virtual High School
Computer Programming Basic 1
Florida Virtual School
Stetson University Virtual School
West Virginia Virtual School
Computer Programming Basic 2
Virtual Greenbush
Computer Programming C++
Electronic High School
Computer Programming I — Java
Electronic High School
Computer Repair 1
York County School Division Virtual High School
Computer Repair 2
York County School Division Virtual High School
Computer Science
Intelligent Education
Michigan Virtual High School
Computer Science — Introduction
NorthStar Academy
Computer Science 1
Clark County School District Virtual High School
Louisiana Virtual School
Computer Skills
Christa McAuliffe Academy
SK Online
Computer Systems Technology 1
York County School Division Virtual High School

Computer Systems Technology 2
York County School Division Virtual High School
Computer Technology
Electronic High School
Computers and the Internet
Delta Cyber School
Computers for Farmers
Intelligent Education
Computers for Learning
Missouri Virtual School
Cyber Basics
Pennsylvania Cyber Charter School
Database Management
Intelligent Education
Design with Photoshop
Laurel Springs School
Desktop Publishing
Delta Cyber School
Intelligent Education
Virtual High School
Digital Communication Systems
Cumberland County Schools' Web Academy
Digital Communication Tools
Evergreen Internet Academy
Digital Geography
Virtual High School
Emergent Computer Technology
James Madison High School Online
Monroe Virtual High School
University of Miami Online High School
Excel XP Core
University of Oklahoma High School
Exploring Computer Science
Virtual High School
HTML Web Design
PA LEARNERS Online Regional Cyber Charter School
HTML with Basic JavaScript
The Potter's School

On Line Academy
Wichita eSchool

Keyboarding 1
Basehor-Linwood Virtual School

Keyboarding 2
Basehor-Linwood Virtual School

Keyboarding and Word Processing
iQ Academies

Keyboarding/Typewriting
Monroe Virtual High School
Pennsylvania Cyber Charter School

Learning Office 03
NorthStar Academy

Logo to Legos
The Potter's School

Media Arts
The Grace Academy
The Jubilee Academy
The MorningStar Academy

Microcomputer Packages
North Dakota Division of
Independent Study

Microsoft Office
Eagle Christian School

Microsoft Office XP
Michigan Virtual High School

MS Office Applications
The Potter's School

MS Office Applications, Level 1
Babbage Net School
Keystone National High School
Pennsylvania Cyber Charter School

Multimedia
Gwinnett County Online Campus
Keystone National High School

Multimedia 1
TRECA Digital Academy

Multimedia Technology
Virtual Community School of Ohio

Multimedia: Digital Photography and Graphics
Keystone National High School

Multimedia: Web Design
Keystone National High School

Networking Basics
Illinois Virtual High School

Office XP
Virtual Community School of Ohio

Personal Keyboarding
Monroe Virtual High School
University of Nebraska-Lincoln
Independent Study High School

PhotoShop
Vilas eSchool

Photoshop Design
Warren County Virtual Community
School

Photoshop Graphics
Delta Cyber School

Pre-A.P. Computer Science
Virtual High School

Principles of CAD
Mississippi Online Learning Institute

Programming in C
West Virginia Virtual School

Programming in C – Algorithms and Techniques
Education Program for Gifted Youth

Programming with Visual Studio .NET
Keystone National High School

Programming: C++ Programming
Keystone National High School

Programming: MS Visual Basic .NET
Keystone National High School

Spreadsheets
Intelligent Education

Technology and Multimedia
Virtual High School

Technology Applications 1
TRECA Digital Academy

Technology Warm-Up
Abaetern Academy

Video Game Development
The Grace Academy

Foreign Languages

The Grace Academy
West Virginia Virtual School

A.P. French Literature
Fairfax County Public Schools
Online Campus

A.P. German
K–12 Distance Learning Academy

A.P. German Language
Intelligent Education
Kentucky Virtual High School

A.P. Greek 1
Scholars' Online Academy

A.P. Latin 4: Catullus and Horacel
Scholars' Online Academy

A.P. Latin 4: Virgil
Scholars' Online Academy

A.P. Latin Literature
Intelligent Education

A.P. Latin: Virgil
Intelligent Education

A.P. Spanish
Clark County School District Virtual
High School
Illinois Virtual High School
iQ Academies
Michigan Virtual High School
Texas Virtual School

A.P. Spanish Language
Fairfax County Public Schools
Online Campus
Intelligent Education
Kentucky Virtual High School
Mississippi Online Learning Institute
Stetson University Virtual School
UC College Prep Online
Virtual Advanced Placement School
Virtual High School
West Virginia Virtual School

A.P. Spanish Literature
Intelligent Education

Advanced Spanish
Eagle Christian School

American Sign Language
Electronic High School

American Sign Language 1
Cyber Oregon Online COOLSchool

American Sign Language 2
Cyber Oregon Online COOLSchool

Ancient Greek 1 Honors
Center for Talent Development

Beginning Spanish
Eagle Christian School

Chinese (Mandarin)
Michigan Virtual High School

Conversational Cultural Spanish
OSU K–12 Online

Danish 1
Electronic High School

Dutch 1
Electronic High School

Dutch 2
Electronic High School

French
Abaetern Academy
Christa McAuliffe Academy
Michigan Virtual High School
North Dakota Division of
Independent Study
PA LEARNERS Online Regional
Cyber Charter School
Trent High School

French 1
American Virtual High School
Babbage Net School
Clark County School District Virtual
High School
Colorado Online Learning
Electronic High School
Elkhart Cyber School
Futures International High School
The Grace Academy
Houston Independent School District
Virtual School
Illinois Virtual High School
Intelligent Education

Delta Cyber School
Electronic High School
Futures International High School
The Grace Academy
Houston Independent School District
Virtual School
Illinois Virtual High School
Indiana University High School
Intelligent Education
iQ Academies
The Jubilee Academy
K–12 Distance Learning Academy
Kentucky Virtual High School
Keystone National High School
Monroe Virtual High School
The MorningStar Academy
Pennsylvania Cyber Charter School
The Potter's School
Virtual Greenbush
West Virginia Virtual School

German 2
Colorado Online Learning
Cumberland County Schools' Web
Academy
Delta Cyber School
Electronic High School
Futures International High School
Gwinnett County Online Campus
Houston Independent School District
Virtual School
Illinois Virtual High School
Intelligent Education
iQ Academies
K–12 Distance Learning Academy
Kentucky Virtual High School
Keystone National High School
Monroe Virtual High School
Pennsylvania Cyber Charter School
The Potter's School
Virtual Greenbush
West Virginia Virtual School

German 3
Intelligent Education
K–12 Distance Learning Academy

Kentucky Virtual High School
Monroe Virtual High School
Pennsylvania Cyber Charter School
West Virginia Virtual School

German 3 Honors
Cumberland County Schools' Web
Academy

German 4
K–12 Distance Learning Academy
Pennsylvania Cyber Charter School

German 4 (Honors)
West Virginia Virtual School

German 4 Honors
Cumberland County Schools' Web
Academy

Greek
Colorado Online Learning

Greek 1
The Potter's School

Greek 2
Scholars' Online Academy
The Potter's School

Greek 3
Scholars' Online Academy

Greek 4
Scholars' Online Academy

Greek 5
Scholars' Online Academy

Greek 6
Scholars' Online Academy

Hebrew 1
American Virtual High School
CompuHigh/Whitmore School
Electronic High School

Hindi 1
Electronic High School

Indonesian 1
Electronic High School

Interactive Spanish 1
University of Missouri-Columbia
High School

Introduction to Sign Language 1
West Virginia Virtual School

Scholars' Online Academy
Stetson University Virtual School
University of Nebraska-Lincoln
  Independent Study High School
USA International On-Line School
Virginia Satellite Educational
  Network
West Virginia Virtual School

Latin 2 Honors
Center for Talent Development

Latin 3
Colorado Online Learning
Electronic High School
Florida Virtual School
Futures International High School
Kentucky Virtual High School
Monroe Virtual High School
Oak Meadow School
Pennsylvania Cyber Charter School
The Potter's School
Regina Coeli Academy
Scholars' Online Academy
Stetson University Virtual School
USA International On-Line School
Virginia Satellite Educational
  Network
West Virginia Virtual School

Latin 3 Honors
Center for Talent Development
Cumberland County Schools' Web
  Academy

Latin 4
Colorado Online Learning
Futures International High School
The Potter's School

Latin 4 Honors
Cumberland County Schools' Web
  Academy

Latin Literature
Kentucky Virtual High School

Medieval Latin
Scholars' Online Academy

Navajo 1
Electronic High School
Navajo 2
Electronic High School
Pashto 1
Electronic High School
Polish 1
Electronic High School
Portuguese 1
Electronic High School
Portuguese 2
Electronic High School
Russian 1
Electronic High School
Intelligent Education
Russian 2
Electronic High School
Intelligent Education
Sign Language
Intelligent Education
Spanish
Abaetern Academy
Blueprint Education
Central Connecticut Adventist
  Virtual School
Christa McAuliffe Academy
Michigan Virtual High School
North Dakota Division of
  Independent Study
Oregon Online
TRECA Digital Academy
Trent High School
Spanish 1
3D Learn
Alabama Online High School
Alpha Omega Academy
American Virtual High School
Babbage Net School
Choice 2000 Online High School
Clark County School District Virtual
  High School
Colorado Online Learning
Colorado State Academy

CompuHigh/Whitmore School
Cumberland County Schools' Web
  Academy
Cyber Oregon Online COOLSchool
Delta Cyber School
Electronic High School
Elkhart Cyber School
E-School
Fairfax County Public Schools
  Online Campus
Florida Virtual School
Futures International High School
The Grace Academy
Houston Independent School District
  Virtual School
Illinois Virtual High School
Intelligent Education
iQ Academies
The Jubilee Academy
K–12 Distance Learning Academy
Karval Online Education
Kentucky Virtual High School
Keystone National High School
Laurel Springs School
Louisiana Virtual School
Minnesota Center of Online Learning
Minnesota Online High School
Mississippi Online Learning Institute
Missouri Virtual School
Monroe Virtual High School
The MorningStar Academy
National University Virtual High
  School
New Jersey Virtual School
NorthStar Academy
Oak Meadow School
On Line Academy
OSU K–12 Online
PA LEARNERS Online Regional
  Cyber Charter School
Pennsylvania Cyber Charter School
Plano ISD eSchool
The Potter's School
Primavera Online High School

Providence High School
SK Online
Stetson University Virtual School
Sycamore Academy
University of Miami Online High
  School
University of Nebraska-Lincoln
  Independent Study High School
University of Oklahoma High School
University of Texas at Austin High
  School
USA International On-Line School
Vilas eSchool
Virtual Community School of Ohio
Virtual Greenbush
Warren County Virtual Community
  School
West Virginia Virtual School
Westside Virtual High School
Wichita eSchool
York County School Division Virtual
  High School

Spanish 2
Alabama Online High School
Alpha Omega Academy
American Virtual High School
Babbage Net School
Choice 2000 Online High School
Colorado Online Learning
Colorado State Academy
CompuHigh/Whitmore School
Cumberland County Schools' Web
  Academy
Cyber Oregon Online COOLSchool
Delta Cyber School
Electronic High School
Elkhart Cyber School
Florida Virtual School
Futures International High School
The Grace Academy
Gwinnett County Online Campus
Houston Independent School District
  Virtual School
Illinois Virtual High School

Intelligent Education
iQ Academies
James Madison High School Online
James Madison High School Online
The Jubilee Academy
K–12 Distance Learning Academy
Karval Online Education
Kentucky Virtual High School
Keystone National High School
Laurel Springs School
Louisiana Virtual School
Minnesota Center of Online Learning
Minnesota Online High School
Missouri Virtual School
Monroe Virtual High School
The MorningStar Academy
National University Virtual High
  School
NorthStar Academy
Oak Meadow School
On Line Academy
OSU K–12 Online
PA LEARNERS Online Regional
  Cyber Charter School
Pennsylvania Cyber Charter School
Plano ISD eSchool
The Potter's School
Providence High School
Stetson University Virtual School
Sycamore Academy
University of Miami Online High
  School
University of Nebraska-Lincoln
  Independent Study High School
University of Oklahoma High School
University of Texas at Austin High
  School
Vilas eSchool
Virtual Community School of Ohio
Virtual Greenbush
Warren County Virtual Community
  School
West Virginia Virtual School
Westside Virtual High School

York County School Division Virtual
  High School

Spanish 2 Honors
Clark County School District Virtual
  High School

Spanish 3
Colorado Online Learning
Futures International High School
Houston Independent School District
  Virtual School
Illinois Virtual High School
Intelligent Education
Kentucky Virtual High School
Louisiana Virtual School
Missouri Virtual School
Monroe Virtual High School
Oak Meadow School
Pennsylvania Cyber Charter School
The Potter's School
University of Nebraska-Lincoln
  Independent Study High School
Virtual Community School of Ohio
Virtual High School@PWCS
Warren County Virtual Community
  School
West Virginia Virtual School
York County School Division Virtual
  High School

Spanish 3 Honors
Cumberland County Schools' Web
  Academy

Spanish 4
Colorado Online Learning
Illinois Virtual High School
Missouri Virtual School
Pennsylvania Cyber Charter School
The Potter's School
SK Online
University of Nebraska-Lincoln
  Independent Study High School

Spanish 4 (Honors)1
West Virginia Virtual School

General Health
  Intelligent Education
Health
  Alpha Omega Academy
  Babbage Net School
  Basehor-Linwood Virtual School
  Central Connecticut Adventist
    Virtual School
  Clark County School District Virtual
    High School
  Colorado Online Learning
  Colorado State Academy
  CompuHigh/Whitmore School
  Delta Cyber School
  Eldorado Academy
  Futures International High School
  James Madison High School Online
  Karval Online Education
  Keystone National High School
  Laurel Springs School
  Maryland Virtual Learning
    Opportunities
  National University Virtual High
    School
  North Dakota Division of
    Independent Study
  Northern Star Online
  On Line Academy
  Oregon Online
  PA LEARNERS Online Regional
    Cyber Charter School
  Pennsylvania Cyber Charter School
  Plano ISD eSchool
  Primavera Online High School
  SK Online
  Sycamore Academy
  Texas Virtual School
  TRECA Digital Academy
  University of Missouri-Columbia
    High School
  Virtual Community School of Ohio
  Virtual High School
  Virtual High School@PWCS

  Warren County Virtual Community
    School
Health 1
  Houston Independent School District
    Virtual School
  OSU K–12 Online
  University of Texas at Austin High
    School
  West Virginia Virtual School
Health and Fitness
  University of Oklahoma High School
Health and Physical Education
  Cumberland County Schools' Web
    Academy
  Georgia Virtual School
  Providence High School
  York County School Division Virtual
    High School
Health and Physical Fitness
  iQ Academies
Health Choices
  Internet Academy
Health Education
  Alabama Online High School
  Blueprint Education
  Indiana University High School
  Monroe Virtual High School
  NorthStar Academy
Health Education 2
  Electronic High School
Health Science
  Illinois Virtual High School
  Michigan Virtual High School
  Minnesota Center of Online Learning
  Monroe Virtual High School
  Northern Star Online
  University of Nebraska-Lincoln
    Independent Study High School
Health Science 1
  Westside Virtual High School
Health Sciences 1
  Virtual Greenbush

Physical Fitness
Blueprint Education
Protecting Yourself from Drugs
Eldorado Academy

Skills for Health
Michigan Virtual High School

Sports Training
National University Virtual High
School

Weight Training
Blueprint Education

Weightlifting for Fitness
Evergreen Internet Academy

Wellness
SK Online

Health Care Professions

First Responder
Gwinnett County Online Campus

Medical Anatomy and Physiology
Electronic High School

Medical Assisting (Honors)
West Virginia Virtual School

Medical Assisting 1
Intelligent Education

Medical Sciences 1
Cumberland County Schools' Web
Academy

Medical Studies
Intelligent Education

Medical Terminology
Intelligent Education

Paramedic Essentials
Intelligent Education

Preveterinary Medicine
Virtual High School

History

A.P. American History
Louisiana Virtual School
Northern Star Online

A.P. European History
Center for Talent Development
Clark County School District Virtual
High School
Cumberland County Schools' Web
Academy
The Grace Academy
Illinois Virtual High School
Intelligent Education
The Jubilee Academy
Kentucky Virtual High School
Mississippi Online Learning Institute
The MorningStar Academy
National University Virtual High
School
Stetson University Virtual School
Virtual Advanced Placement School
York County School Division Virtual
High School

A.P. U.S. History
Center for Talent Development
Christa McAuliffe Academy
Clark County School District Virtual
High School
Cumberland County Schools' Web
Academy
Fairfax County Public Schools
Online Campus
The Grace Academy
Illinois Virtual High School
Intelligent Education
iQ Academies
The Jubilee Academy
Michigan Virtual High School
Missouri Virtual School
Monroe Virtual High School
The MorningStar Academy
National University Virtual High
School
Stetson University Virtual School
Texas Virtual School
UC College Prep Online
University of Miami Online High
School

Ancient History
3D Learn

Ancient History: Along the Nile and Around the Mediterranean
The Potter's School

Ancient World Civilizations
Electronic High School

Bible as History
Cumberland County Schools' Web Academy

Church History 2
Regina Coeli Academy

The Civil War in Depth
On Line Academy

College Preparatory U.S. History
Gwinnett County Online Campus

College Preparatory World History
Gwinnett County Online Campus

Colorado History
Colorado Online Learning

Days of the Knights: Medieval Times
The Potter's School

Early U.S. History
Trent High School

European History and English
3D Learn

Exploring U.S. History
Virtual High School

Global History
The Francis School

The Golden Age of Classical Greece
Virtual High School

History and Culture of the American West
The Potter's School

History of America
Warren County Virtual Community School

History of Asia
Intelligent Education

History of Asia (Honors)
Intelligent Education

West Virginia Virtual School

History of Egypt and Canaan
Intelligent Education

History of Medieval Britain
Intelligent Education

History of Religion
Intelligent Education

History of the Crusades
Intelligent Education

History of the Crusades (Honors)
West Virginia Virtual School

History of the Holocaust
Intelligent Education

History of the Holocaust (Honors)
West Virginia Virtual School

History of the World
The Potter's School
Warren County Virtual Community School

History of the World 1
Karval Online Education

History of the World 2
Karval Online Education

History of U.S. Constitution
Colorado State Academy

History/Civics
Trent High School

The Holocaust
Virtual High School

Indians of Missouri
Monroe Virtual High School
Pennsylvania Cyber Charter School

Kansas History
Virtual Greenbush

King Arthur and the Middle Ages
Monroe Virtual High School
Pennsylvania Cyber Charter School

Lewis and Clark's Expedition
Virtual High School

Local History
North Dakota Division of Independent Study

UC College Prep Online
University of Texas at Austin High
    School
Virtual High School
**U.S. History – Colonial Through
Civil War**
NorthStar Academy
**U.S. History – Reconstruction to
Present**
NorthStar Academy
U.S. History 1
New Jersey Virtual School
Northern Star Online
Wichita eSchool
U.S. History 2
Electronic High School
New Jersey Virtual School
Northern Star Online
Wichita eSchool
U.S. History 3
Evergreen Internet Academy
U.S. History 4
Evergreen Internet Academy
U.S. History and Government
E-School
U.S. History Honors
Center for Talent Development
**U.S. History Studies Since
Reconstruction**
Houston Independent School District
    Virtual School
U.S. Military History
Futures International High School
The Vietnam War
Virtual High School
Virginia and U.S. History
York County School Division Virtual
    High School
Western Civilization
The Potter's School
NorthStar Academy
Intelligent Education

Eldorado Academy
Delta Cyber School
Western Civilization Honors
Intelligent Education
World Civilizations 1
Virtual Greenbush
World History
Alpha Omega Academy
Babbage Net School
Basehor-Linwood Virtual School
Blueprint Education
Central Connecticut Adventist
    Virtual School
Choice 2000 Online High School
Christa McAuliffe Academy
Clark County School District Virtual
    High School
Clintondale Virtual High School
Colorado Online Learning
Colorado State Academy
Cumberland County Schools' Web
    Academy
Cyber Oregon Online COOLSchool
Elkhart Cyber School
Florida Virtual School
Futures International High School
Georgia Virtual School
The Grace Academy
Illinois Virtual High School
Indiana University High School
Intelligent Education
Internet Academy
Internet High School
iQ Academies
James Madison High School Online
The Jubilee Academy
Keystone National High School
Laurel Springs School
Louisiana Virtual School
Michigan Virtual High School
Monroe Virtual High School
The MorningStar Academy

Language Arts

10th Grade Literature and Composition
Georgia Virtual School

9th Grade Literature and Composition
Georgia Virtual School

A Journey Through Narnia
The Potter's School

A.P. Creative Writing
Missouri Virtual School

A.P. English
Delta Cyber School
Eagle Christian School
iQ Academies
Scholars' Online Academy
Virginia Satellite Educational Network
York County School Division Virtual High School

A.P. English Language (Honors)
West Virginia Virtual School

A.P. English Language and Composition
Center for Talent Development
Clark County School District Virtual High School
Cumberland County Schools' Web Academy
Education Program for Gifted Youth
Fairfax County Public Schools Online Campus
Florida Virtual School
Georgia Virtual School
The Grace Academy
Illinois Virtual High School
The Jubilee Academy
Kentucky Virtual High School
Mississippi Online Learning Institute
Monroe Virtual High School
The MorningStar Academy
Stetson University Virtual School
Texas Virtual School

UC College Prep Online
University of Miami Online High School
Virtual Advanced Placement School
Virtual Greenbush
Virtual High School
West Virginia Virtual School

A.P. English Literature and Composition
Center for Talent Development
Colorado Online Learning
Cumberland County Schools' Web Academy
Cyber Oregon Online COOLSchool
Fairfax County Public Schools Online Campus
Florida Virtual School
The Grace Academy
Gwinnett County Online Campus
Illinois Virtual High School
Intelligent Education
The Jubilee Academy
Kentucky Virtual High School
Maryland Virtual Learning Opportunities
Mississippi Online Learning Institute
Monroe Virtual High School
The MorningStar Academy
New Jersey Virtual School
Stetson University Virtual School
Texas Virtual School
University of Miami Online High School
University of Missouri-Columbia High School
Virtual Advanced Placement School
Virtual Greenbush
West Virginia Virtual School

Academic Writing Section
Virtual High School

Adult Composition
Colorado State Academy

Adult Grammar
Colorado State Academy

Warren County Virtual Community
School

American Literature Studies
Monroe Virtual High School
University of Nebraska-Lincoln
Independent Study High School

**American Literature: Society and
Developing Identities**
Monroe Virtual High School
University of Missouri-Columbia
High School

The American Short Story
Monroe Virtual High School
University of Nebraska-Lincoln
Independent Study High School

Applied Communications
Clark County School District Virtual
High School

Basic Composition
Indiana University High School
Monroe Virtual High School

Basic English
Providence High School

Basic English Grammar
American Virtual High School

Basic Expository Writing
Monroe Virtual High School
University of Nebraska-Lincoln
Independent Study High School

Basic Grammar
CompuHigh/Whitmore School
Monroe Virtual High School
University of Nebraska-Lincoln
Independent Study High School

Basic Reading Skills
Virtual Community School of Ohio

Basic Vocabulary
Monroe Virtual High School

Basic Writing Skills
Virtual Community School of Ohio

Beginning Composition
Illinois Virtual High School
iQ Academies

Michigan Virtual High School
Virtual Greenbush
Westside Virtual High School

**Beginning Composition: A Writing
Road Trip**
West Virginia Virtual School

Beginning Comprehension
Minnesota Center of Online Learning

Beginning Writing for Publications
Eagle Christian School

The Bible as Literature
Monroe Virtual High School

British Literature
Christa McAuliffe Academy
Eagle Christian School
Elkhart Cyber School
Intelligent Education
James Madison High School Online
Laurel Springs School
Maryland Virtual Learning
Opportunities
Minnesota Online High School
National University Virtual High
School
North Dakota Division of
Independent Study
NorthStar Academy
PA LEARNERS Online Regional
Cyber Charter School
Pennsylvania Cyber Charter School
The Potter's School
University of Miami Online High
School
West Virginia Virtual School

British Literature 12
Primavera Online High School

British Literature Honors
University of Miami Online High
School
Warren County Virtual Community
School

**Building English Vocabulary from
Latin and Greek Roots**
The Potter's School

Composition with Grammar Review
Monroe Virtual High School

Contemporary American Poetry
Virtual High School

Contemporary Authors
3D Learn

Contemporary English
Blueprint Education

Contemporary Irish Literature
Virtual High School

Conversational English
Virtual Greenbush
Westside Virtual High School

Corrective English
Portland State University
Independent Study

Creative Writing
Abaetern Academy
Alabama Online High School
Babbage Net School
Delta Cyber School
Evergreen Internet Academy
Fairfax County Public Schools
Online Campus
The Grace Academy
Illinois Virtual High School
Internet Academy
Internet High School
The Jubilee Academy
Keystone National High School
Laurel Springs School
Minnesota Center of Online Learning
Missouri Virtual School
Monroe Virtual High School
The MorningStar Academy
North Dakota Division of
Independent Study
NorthStar Academy
On Line Academy
OSU K–12 Online
Pennsylvania Cyber Charter School
South Dakota Virtual Campus
TRECA Digital Academy

University of Missouri-Columbia
High School
Virtual Greenbush
Virtual High School@PWCS
Warren County Virtual Community
School

**Creative Writing for People Who
Mean It**
Virtual High School

Creative Writing Honors
Center for Talent Development

Creative Writing: Fiction
Indiana University High School
Monroe Virtual High School

**Cross-curricular English
Composition**
Regina Coeli Academy
Scholars' Online Academy

Developmental English
North Dakota Division of
Independent Study

Developmental Reading
Monroe Virtual High School

**Directed Study in English Language
Arts**
E-School

Drama
Virtual Community School of Ohio
Eldorado Academy
Choice 2000 Online High School
Christa McAuliffe Academy

Drama in Literature
Laurel Springs School
Warren County Virtual Community
School

Drama in Literature Honors
Laurel Springs School
Warren County Virtual Community
School

Dramatic Script Writing Honors
Center for Talent Development

Early American Literature
The Potter's School

The Grace Academy
Indiana University High School
Intelligent Education
Internet Academy
Internet High School
iQ Academies
The Jubilee Academy
Michigan Virtual High School
Monroe Virtual High School
The MorningStar Academy
National University Virtual High
  School
Oak Meadow School
Pennsylvania Cyber Charter School
Portland State University
  Independent Study
Texas Tech University Extended
  Studies
Trent High School
UC College Prep Online
University of Missouri-Columbia
  High School
University of Nebraska-Lincoln
  Independent Study High School
University of Oklahoma High School
Virtual Greenbush
Virtual High School
Virtual High School@PWCS
York County School Division Virtual
  High School

English 10 Honors
Internet Academy
iQ Academies

English 11
Alabama Online High School
American Virtual High School
CompuHigh/Whitmore School
Electronic High School
Fairfax County Public Schools
  Online Campus
Futures International High School
The Grace Academy
Internet Academy
Internet High School

iQ Academies
The Jubilee Academy
Michigan Virtual High School
Monroe Virtual High School
The MorningStar Academy
National University Virtual High
  School
Pennsylvania Cyber Charter School
Portland State University
  Independent Study
South Dakota Virtual Campus
Texas Tech University Extended
  Studies
Trent High School
UC College Prep Online
University of Missouri-Columbia
  High School
University of Nebraska-Lincoln
  Independent Study High School
University of Oklahoma High School
Virtual Greenbush
Virtual High School@PWCS
York County School Division Virtual
  High School

English 11 Honors
iQ Academies

English 12
Alabama Online High School
American Virtual High School
CompuHigh/Whitmore School
Electronic High School
Fairfax County Public Schools
  Online Campus
Futures International High School
The Grace Academy
Internet High School
iQ Academies
The Jubilee Academy
Michigan Virtual High School
Monroe Virtual High School
The MorningStar Academy
National University Virtual High
  School
Pennsylvania Cyber Charter School

University of Miami Online High School

University of Texas at Austin High School

USA International On-Line School

Vilas eSchool

West Virginia Virtual School

Wichita eSchool

English 3 Honors

Cumberland County Schools' Web Academy

Florida Virtual School

Keystone National High School

Monroe Virtual High School

Stetson University Virtual School

University of Miami Online High School

USA International On-Line School

English 4

Babbage Net School

Basehor-Linwood Virtual School

Choice 2000 Online High School

Cumberland County Schools' Web Academy

Delta Cyber School

Florida Virtual School

The Francis School

Houston Independent School District Virtual School

Karval Online Education

Kentucky Virtual High School

Keystone National High School

Louisiana Virtual School

Monroe Virtual High School

New Jersey Virtual School

On Line Academy

Pinnacle Education Virtual School

Plano ISD eSchool

Providence High School

Stetson University Virtual School

TRECA Digital Academy

University of Miami Online High School

University of Texas at Austin High School

USA International On-Line School

Vilas eSchool

West Virginia Virtual School

English 4 Honors

Cumberland County Schools' Web Academy

Florida Virtual School

Monroe Virtual High School

Stetson University Virtual School

University of Miami Online High School

USA International On-Line School

English 9

Alabama Online High School

American Virtual High School

CompuHigh/Whitmore School

Electronic High School

Evergreen Internet Academy

Fairfax County Public Schools Online Campus

Futures International High School

The Grace Academy

Indiana University High School

Intelligent Education

Internet Academy

Internet High School

iQ Academies

The Jubilee Academy

Michigan Virtual High School

Monroe Virtual High School

The MorningStar Academy

National University Virtual High School

Northern Star Online

Oak Meadow School

Pennsylvania Cyber Charter School

Portland State University Independent Study

South Dakota Virtual Campus

Texas Tech University Extended Studies

Trent High School

UC College Prep Online

The Experience of Drama
Indiana University High School

Exploring English Literature
Virtual High School

Expository Writing
NorthStar Academy
West Virginia Virtual School

Fantasy Literature
The Potter's School

Fantasy Writing
3D Learn

The Fellowship of the Ring
Laurel Springs School

Fiction
Abaetern Academy

Fiction Literature
West Virginia Virtual School

Five Novels of Change
Monroe Virtual High School

Folklore and Literature of Myth, Magic, and Ritual
Virtual High School

Foundations of Language Arts
Alpha Omega Academy

Freshman Language and Composition
North Dakota Division of
Independent Study

Freshman Literature
North Dakota Division of
Independent Study

Fundamentals of English 9
Primavera Online High School

Fundamentals of Public Speaking
North Dakota Division of
Independent Study

Gateway Reading and Literary Analysis
Virtual High School

Gateway Writing
Virtual High School

Grammar and Composition
Babbage Net School
Keystone National High School

Grammar and Style
NorthStar Academy

Grammar and Style of the Sentence
Education Program for Gifted Youth

Grammar and Writing Mechanics
Eldorado Academy

Grammar Review and Compositional Writing
The Potter's School

Grammar, Language, Spelling, and Vocabulary
Pennsylvania Cyber Charter School

Grammar, Spelling, and Vocabulary
Monroe Virtual High School

Great Books
Eagle Christian School

Greek and Roman Literature in Translation
The Potter's School

Greek Mythology
NorthStar Academy

Hearts of Darkness
Virtual High School

Her Stories: Women's Voices in American Literature
Monroe Virtual High School
University of Missouri-Columbia
High School

Heroes
Virtual High School

High School Reading
Basehor-Linwood Virtual School

Horror, Mystery and Science Fiction Literature
Virtual High School

Independent Study: English
OSU K–12 Online

Intermediate Essay Writing
West Virginia Virtual School

Library Science
Cumberland County Schools' Web Academy

Literary Analysis Honors
Center for Talent Development

Literary Elements
Eldorado Academy

Literature for Reluctant Readers
North Dakota Division of Independent Study

Literature of America
Warren County Virtual Community School

Literature of the Future
Indiana University High School
Monroe Virtual High School

Literature of the World
Warren County Virtual Community School

Major Authors
Eldorado Academy

Man vs. Nature in Literature
Virtual Greenbush

Mastering Composition Through Grammar
Regina Coeli Academy
Scholars' Online Academy

Material Logic/Rhetoric
Regina Coeli Academy

Mexican American Literature
Intelligent Education

Mexican American Literature Honors
Intelligent Education

Mexican-American Literature
West Virginia Virtual School

Modern Fiction and Nonfiction
Eldorado Academy

Modern Literature
Clark County School District Virtual High School

Multicultural Literature
Monroe Virtual High School

University of Nebraska-Lincoln Independent Study High School

Multicultural Themes in Literature
Clark County School District Virtual High School

Mysteries
Monroe Virtual High School

Mystery Fiction
Monroe Virtual High School
Pennsylvania Cyber Charter School

Mythology
Evergreen Internet Academy
Indiana University High School
Laurel Springs School
Monroe Virtual High School
North Dakota Division of Independent Study
Pennsylvania Cyber Charter School
Virtual High School
Warren County Virtual Community School

Native American Literature
CompuHigh/Whitmore School
Intelligent Education
West Virginia Virtual School

Native American Literature Honors
Intelligent Education

Nonfiction Literature
Eldorado Academy

Non-Fiction Writing Honors
Center for Talent Development

Novels
Eldorado Academy

Online Journalism
James Madison High School Online
University of Miami Online High School

Oregon Writers
Cyber Oregon Online COOLSchool

Periods of English Literature
Eldorado Academy

Poetry
Abaetern Academy

Science Fiction Literature
Intelligent Education
The Potter's School

Science Fiction Literature (Honors)
West Virginia Virtual School

Science Fiction/Fantasy
Evergreen Internet Academy

Science in Literature
Colorado Online Learning

Screenwriting Fundamentals
Virtual High School

Search for Identity Through Literature
Monroe Virtual High School
Pennsylvania Cyber Charter School

Senior Composition
South Dakota Virtual Campus

Senior Language and Composition
North Dakota Division of Independent Study

Senior Year Composition (Advanced Composition)
Monroe Virtual High School

Shakespeare
Choice 2000 Online High School
Internet Academy
The Potter's School

Shakespearean Literature
Laurel Springs School
Warren County Virtual Community School

Shakespearean Literature Honors
Laurel Springs School
Warren County Virtual Community School

Shakespearean Theater: The Comedies
Colorado Online Learning

Shakespearean Theater: The Tragedies
Colorado Online Learning

Short Stories
Eldorado Academy
Blueprint Education

Short Stories for Reluctant Readers
Monroe Virtual High School

The Short Story
Indiana University High School
Monroe Virtual High School

Sophomore Language and Composition
North Dakota Division of Independent Study

Sophomore Literature
North Dakota Division of Independent Study

Sophomore Survey 1 – Literature Survey
SK Online

Sophomore Survey 1 – Writers' Workshop
SK Online

Speak Your Mind
Monroe Virtual High School
Pennsylvania Cyber Charter School

Speech
American Virtual High School
Blueprint Education
CompuHigh/Whitmore School
Elkhart Cyber School
Monroe Virtual High School

Stories to Live By
Providence High School

Structure of Grammar and Genres of Literature
Alpha Omega Academy

Structure of Writing
PA LEARNERS Online Regional Cyber Charter School

Survey of Literature
James Madison High School Online

Survey of World Drama
York County School Division Virtual High School

Writing Process
Northern Star Online
Writing Tutorials
Laurel Springs School
Warren County Virtual Community
School
Writing With Style
Cyber Oregon Online COOLSchool
Young Adult Literature
Virtual High School

Legal Studies

Business and Personal Law
Monroe Virtual High School
Pennsylvania Cyber Charter School
Virtual High School
Business Law
Babbage Net School
Basehor-Linwood Virtual School
Blueprint Education
Clark County School District Virtual
High School
Cumberland County Schools' Web
Academy
Electronic High School
Gwinnett County Online Campus
Internet Academy
Keystone National High School
Monroe Virtual High School
Pennsylvania Cyber Charter School
University of Nebraska-Lincoln
Independent Study High School
York County School Division Virtual
High School
Civil and Criminal Law
On Line Academy
Constitutional Law
The Potter's School
Virtual High School
Consumer Law
Colorado Online Learning
Criminal and Consumer Law

Pennsylvania Cyber Charter School
Ethics and Law
Gwinnett County Online Campus
**Introduction to Business and
Personal Law**
Intelligent Education
Introduction to Law
The Grace Academy
The Jubilee Academy
The MorningStar Academy
Introduction to Paralegal Studies
Intelligent Education
**Introduction to Paralegal Studies
(Honors)**
West Virginia Virtual School
**Introduction to Personal and
Business Law**
Intelligent Education
Law
Gwinnett County Online Campus
Law and Justice
North Dakota Division of
Independent Study
Law in America
Monroe Virtual High School
Legal Issues
Michigan Virtual High School
Legal Research/Writing
Intelligent Education
Legal Studies
Intelligent Education
Medical and Legal Ethics
Intelligent Education
Practical Law
Virtual High School
Street Law
Elkhart Cyber School
You and the Law
Monroe Virtual High School
University of Missouri-Columbia
High School

Mathematics

A.P. Calculus
Colorado Online Learning
Cumberland County Schools' Web
   Academy
Cyber Oregon Online COOLSchool
Michigan Virtual High School
NorthStar Academy
University of Miami Online High
   School
Virginia Satellite Educational
   Network
West Virginia Virtual School
Wichita eSchool

A.P. Calculus AB
Center for Talent Development
Evergreen Internet Academy
Fairfax County Public Schools
   Online Campus
Florida Virtual School
Georgia Virtual School
Gwinnett County Online Campus
Illinois Virtual High School
iQ Academies
K–12 Distance Learning Academy
Kentucky Virtual High School
Maryland Virtual Learning
   Opportunities
Mississippi Online Learning Institute
Missouri Virtual School
Monroe Virtual High School
Stetson University Virtual School
Texas Virtual School
UC College Prep Online
Virtual High School
West Virginia Virtual School

A.P. Calculus BC
Center for Talent Development
Clark County School District Virtual
   High School
Intelligent Education
iQ Academies
Kentucky Virtual High School

The Potter's School
UC College Prep Online
Virtual High School

A.P. Statistics
Center for Talent Development
Clark County School District Virtual
   High School
Fairfax County Public Schools
   Online Campus
Gwinnett County Online Campus
Illinois Virtual High School
Intelligent Education
Kentucky Virtual High School
Maryland Virtual Learning
   Opportunities
Michigan Virtual High School
Northern Star Online
Texas Virtual School
UC College Prep Online
Virginia Satellite Educational
   Network
Virtual High School
West Virginia Virtual School

Accelerated Algebra 2/Trigonometry
Gwinnett County Online Campus

Advanced Algebra
Monroe Virtual High School
Regina Coeli Academy
SK Online
University of Nebraska-Lincoln
   Independent Study High School

Advanced Algebra 1
The Potter's School

Advanced Algebra and Trigonometry
Georgia Virtual School
Gwinnett County Online Campus

Advanced Functions and Modeling
Cumberland County Schools' Web
   Academy

Advanced Math
Eagle Christian School
Oak Meadow School

TRECA Digital Academy
Virtual Community School of Ohio

**Advanced Mathematical Concepts 1
with Trigonometry**
Trent High School

**Advanced Mathematical Concepts 2
with Trigonometry and Introduction
to Calculus**
Trent High School

Advanced Mathematics
Louisiana Virtual School

Advanced Middle Math 1
Northern Star Online

Advanced Middle Math 2
Northern Star Online

Algebra
Abaetern Academy
Blueprint Education
Clintondale Virtual High School
Michigan Virtual High School
North Dakota Division of
Independent Study
Oregon Online
The Potter's School
QualitySchoolHouse
Texas Tech University Extended
Studies
Trent High School

Algebra 1
3D Learn
Alabama Online High School
Alpha Omega Academy
American Virtual High School
Babbage Net School
Basehor-Linwood Virtual School
Central Connecticut Adventist
Virtual School
Choice 2000 Online High School
Christa McAuliffe Academy
Clark County School District Virtual
High School
Colorado Online Learning
CompuHigh/Whitmore School

Cumberland County Schools' Web
Academy
Cyber Oregon Online COOLSchool
Delta Cyber School
Eagle Christian School
Eldorado Academy
Elkhart Cyber School
E-School
Evergreen Internet Academy
Fairfax County Public Schools
Online Campus
Florida Virtual School
Futures International High School
Georgia Virtual School
The Grace Academy
Gwinnett County Online Campus
Houston Independent School District
Virtual School
Illinois Virtual High School
Intelligent Education
Internet Academy
Internet High School
Internet Home School
iQ Academies
James Madison High School Online
The Jubilee Academy
Karval Online Education
Kentucky Virtual High School
Keystone National High School
Laurel Springs School
Louisiana Virtual School
Minnesota Center of Online Learning
Minnesota Online High School
Monroe Virtual High School
Monroe Virtual High School
The MorningStar Academy
National University Virtual High
School
New Jersey Virtual School
Northern Star Online
NorthStar Academy
Oak Meadow School
On Line Academy
OSU K–12 Online

Internet High School
Internet Home School
iQ Academies
James Madison High School Online
The Jubilee Academy
Karval Online Education
Kentucky Virtual High School
Keystone National High School
Laurel Springs School
Minnesota Center of Online Learning
Minnesota Online High School
Mississippi Online Learning Institute
Monroe Virtual High School
The MorningStar Academy
National University Virtual High
  School
New Jersey Virtual School
Northern Star Online
NorthStar Academy
Oak Meadow School
On Line Academy
PA LEARNERS Online Regional
  Cyber Charter School
Pennsylvania Cyber Charter School
Plano ISD eSchool
Primavera Online High School
Providence High School
SK Online
Stetson University Virtual School
Sycamore Academy
TRECA Digital Academy
Trent High School
University of Miami Online High
  School
University of Missouri-Columbia
  High School
University of Oklahoma High School
University of Texas at Austin High
  School
USA International On-Line School
Victory Math
Vilas eSchool
Virtual Community School of Ohio
Virtual Greenbush

Virtual High School
Virtual High School@PWCS
Warren County Virtual Community
  School
Westside Virtual High School
Wichita eSchool
York County School Division Virtual
  High School

Algebra 2 Honors
Center for Talent Development
Florida Virtual School
Stetson University Virtual School
University of Miami Online High
  School
USA International On-Line School

Algebra 2 with Saxon
The Grace Academy
The Jubilee Academy
The MorningStar Academy
Victory Math

Algebra 2/Statistics
Trent High School

Algebra 2/Trigonometry
Christa McAuliffe Academy

Algebra 3
Evergreen Internet Academy
Georgia Virtual School
Internet Academy

Algebra 4
Evergreen Internet Academy
Internet Academy

Algebra and Data Analysis
Maryland Virtual Learning
  Opportunities

Analytic Geometry and Calculus
Missouri Virtual School

Applied Business Math
Oak Meadow School

Applied Math
Delta Cyber School
Monroe Virtual High School

Arithmetic
Eagle Christian School

Calculus for Business
Virtual High School

College Algebra
Missouri Virtual School
North Dakota Division of
Independent Study

Concepts of Algebra
Gwinnett County Online Campus

Concepts of Problem Solving
Gwinnett County Online Campus

Consumer Math
Babbage Net School
Blueprint Education
Choice 2000 Online High School
Colorado State Academy
Delta Cyber School
Eagle Christian School
Elkhart Cyber School
Futures International High School
The Grace Academy
Internet High School
The Jubilee Academy
Keystone National High School
The MorningStar Academy
North Dakota Division of
Independent Study
Oak Meadow School
On Line Academy
Providence High School
Sycamore Academy
TRECA Digital Academy
Victory Math

Contemporary Math 1
Clark County School District Virtual
High School

Core IIA (9)
Northern Star Online

Core IIIA (10)
Northern Star Online

Discrete Math
Gwinnett County Online Campus

Elementary Algebra
North Dakota Division of
Independent Study

Electronic High School

Euclidean Geometry
Georgia Virtual School

Exploring Geometry
Northern Star Online

Exploring Statistics
Virtual High School

First Year Algebra
University of Nebraska-Lincoln
Independent Study High School

Fractals
Virtual High School

Function and Trigonometry
Sycamore Academy

**Functions, Statistics, and
Trigonometry**
The Potter's School

**Functions: Statistics and
Trigonometry**
Northern Star Online

Fundamental Math
Colorado Online Learning

Game Theory
National University Virtual High
School

Gateway Math
Virtual High School

General Math
Blueprint Education
Clintondale Virtual High School
Delta Cyber School
Monroe Virtual High School
North Dakota Division of
Independent Study
Portland State University
Independent Study
SK Online
University of Missouri-Columbia
High School
University of Nebraska-Lincoln
Independent Study High School
University of Oklahoma High School

Virtual High School@PWCS
Warren County Virtual Community
School
West Virginia Virtual School
Wichita eSchool
York County School Division Virtual
High School

Geometry 1
Alpha Omega Academy
Cyber Oregon Online COOLSchool
Plano ISD eSchool
Portland State University
Independent Study
Virtual Greenbush
Westside Virtual High School

Geometry 1 – Integrated
Evergreen Internet Academy

Geometry 2
Portland State University
Independent Study

Geometry 2 – Integrated
Evergreen Internet Academy

Geometry Honors
Center for Talent Development
Education Program for Gifted Youth
Florida Virtual School
iQ Academies
Stetson University Virtual School
University of Miami Online High
School
USA International On-Line School
West Virginia Virtual School

Honors Algebra 2
iQ Academies

Honors Beginning Algebra
Education Program for Gifted Youth

Honors Intermediate Algebra
Education Program for Gifted Youth

Honors Precalculus
Education Program for Gifted Youth

**Honors Precalculus and
Trigonometry**
iQ Academies

Informal Geometry
Gwinnett County Online Campus
Wichita eSchool

Integrated
The Grace Academy
The Jubilee Academy
The MorningStar Academy
Victory Math

Integrated Math 1
TRECA Digital Academy

Integrated Math 2
TRECA Digital Academy

Integrated Mathematics
Monroe Virtual High School

Intermediate Algebra
Electronic High School
Missouri Virtual School
North Dakota Division of
Independent Study

Introduction to Advanced Algebra
SK Online

Introduction to Algebra
Virtual Community School of Ohio

Introduction to Calculus
Clintondale Virtual High School

Introduction to Statistics
Trent High School

Liberal Arts Math
Florida Virtual School
Stetson University Virtual School

Logic 1
NorthStar Academy

Logic 2
NorthStar Academy

Math 1
Virtual Community School of Ohio

Math 10
Colorado State Academy

Math 11
Colorado State Academy

Math 12
Colorado State Academy

Elkhart Cyber School
Intelligent Education
iQ Academies
Karval Online Education
Kentucky Virtual High School
Keystone National High School
Michigan Virtual High School
Minnesota Center of Online Learning
Minnesota Online High School
National University Virtual High
 School
On Line Academy
Oregon Online
OSU K–12 Online
PA LEARNERS Online Regional
 Cyber Charter School
Pennsylvania Cyber Charter School
Pinnacle Education Virtual School
Plano ISD eSchool
Primavera Online High School
Providence High School
University of Miami Online High
 School
USA International On-Line School
Vilas eSchool
Virtual Greenbush
Warren County Virtual Community
 School
Westside Virtual High School
Wichita eSchool

Prealgebra 1
Electronic High School

Precalculus
Alpha Omega Academy
Babbage Net School
Clark County School District Virtual
 High School
Colorado Online Learning
Cyber Oregon Online COOLSchool
Delta Cyber School
Electronic High School
Florida Virtual School
Futures International High School

Houston Independent School District
 Virtual School
Illinois Virtual High School
Intelligent Education
James Madison High School Online
Kentucky Virtual High School
Keystone National High School
Michigan Virtual High School
Missouri Virtual School
Monroe Virtual High School
National University Virtual High
 School
NorthStar Academy
On Line Academy
Oregon Online
PA LEARNERS Online Regional
 Cyber Charter School
Pennsylvania Cyber Charter School
Plano ISD eSchool
Regina Coeli Academy
SK Online
Stetson University Virtual School
University of Miami Online High
 School
University of Nebraska-Lincoln
 Independent Study High School
University of Texas at Austin High
 School
USA International On-Line School
Virtual Greenbush
West Virginia Virtual School
Westside Virtual High School
Wichita eSchool

Precalculus 1
Minnesota Center of Online Learning

Precalculus and Analytic Geometry
University of Oklahoma High School

**Precalculus and Discrete
Mathematics**
The Potter's School

Precalculus and Trigonometry
iQ Academies

Precalculus Honors
Center for Talent Development

Religion

The Jubilee Academy
The MorningStar Academy
Bible 12: Solid Ground Theology
The Grace Academy
The Jubilee Academy
The MorningStar Academy
Bible 2
Central Connecticut Adventist
   Virtual School
Bible 9: New Testament
The Grace Academy
The Jubilee Academy
The MorningStar Academy
Bible Doctrine and Theology
The Potter's School
Bible Study 10
Colorado State Academy
Bible Study 11
Colorado State Academy
Bible Study 12
Colorado State Academy
Bible Study 9
Colorado State Academy
Christian Evangelism
The Grace Academy
The Jubilee Academy
The MorningStar Academy
Christian Manhood
The Grace Academy
The Jubilee Academy
The MorningStar Academy
Christian Womanhood
The Grace Academy
The Jubilee Academy
The MorningStar Academy
Confirmation
Regina Coeli Academy
Cultural Immersion
NorthStar Academy
Eastern and Western Thought
Virtual High School

Faith and Literature
The Potter's School
Forming Your Biblical Worldview
The Potter's School
God and Government: Advanced Government and Biblical Perspectives
The Potter's School
God in All Worlds
The Potter's School
Homiletics
Eagle Christian School
Isaiah and Creation
NorthStar Academy
Isaiah and the Bible
NorthStar Academy
Life in Christ
Eagle Christian School
New Testament Survey
Eagle Christian School
NorthStar Academy
Old Testament Survey
Eagle Christian School
NorthStar Academy
Social Action
The Grace Academy
The Jubilee Academy
The MorningStar Academy
Survey of Bible History and Culture
The Potter's School
Theology 1
Regina Coeli Academy
Theology 2
Regina Coeli Academy
Theology 3
Regina Coeli Academy
Theology 4
Regina Coeli Academy

Science

A.P. Biology

Center for Talent Development

Clark County School District Virtual High School

Cumberland County Schools' Web Academy

Fairfax County Public Schools Online Campus

Florida Virtual School

Georgia Virtual School

The Grace Academy

Illinois Virtual High School

Intelligent Education

iQ Academies

The Jubilee Academy

Kentucky Virtual High School

Michigan Virtual High School

Monroe Virtual High School

The MorningStar Academy

National University Virtual High School

New Jersey Virtual School

NorthStar Academy

OSU K–12 Online

Stetson University Virtual School

Texas Virtual School

UC College Prep Online

University of Miami Online High School

Virtual Advanced Placement School

Virtual High School

Virtual High School@PWCS

West Virginia Virtual School

A.P. Chemistry

Center for Talent Development

Clark County School District Virtual High School

Cumberland County Schools' Web Academy

Cyber Oregon Online COOLSchool

Fairfax County Public Schools Online Campus

Illinois Virtual High School

Intelligent Education

iQ Academies

Kentucky Virtual High School

Michigan Virtual High School

National University Virtual High School

NorthStar Academy

Texas Virtual School

University of Miami Online High School

Virtual Advanced Placement School

Virtual High School

West Virginia Virtual School

York County School Division Virtual High School

A.P. Enviromental Science

Center for Talent Development

Cumberland County Schools' Web Academy

Illinois Virtual High School

Intelligent Education

Kentucky Virtual High School

UC College Prep Online

Virtual High School

A.P. Physics

Cumberland County Schools' Web Academy

Intelligent Education

iQ Academies

Michigan Virtual High School

Mississippi Online Learning Institute

New Jersey Virtual School

A.P. Physics A and B

Texas Virtual School

A.P. Physics B

Center for Talent Development

Clark County School District Virtual High School

Fairfax County Public Schools Online Campus

Georgia Virtual School

Illinois Virtual High School

Kentucky Virtual High School

Maryland Virtual Learning
 Opportunities
UC College Prep Online
Virtual Advanced Placement School
Virtual High School
West Virginia Virtual School
A.P. Physics C
Center for Talent Development
Clark County School District Virtual
 High School
Illinois Virtual High School
Intelligent Education
UC College Prep Online
Virtual High School
**A.P. Physics C: Electricity and
Magnetism**
West Virginia Virtual School
A.P. Physics C: Mechanics
West Virginia Virtual School
Acoustics
Abaetern Academy
Active Galactic Nuclei
Abaetern Academy
Adult Science
Colorado State Academy
Advanced Biology
Elkhart Cyber School
Advanced Biology Themes
Primavera Online High School
Advanced Chemistry in Creation
The Potter's School
Advanced Physics in Creation
The Potter's School
**Aerospace: Crossing the Space
Frontier**
Monroe Virtual High School
Pennsylvania Cyber Charter School
University of Missouri-Columbia
 High School
Agriscience
Monroe Virtual High School
University of Nebraska-Lincoln
 Independent Study High School

Anatomy and Physiology
Colorado Online Learning
CompuHigh/Whitmore School
Cumberland County Schools' Web
 Academy
Delta Cyber School
Eagle Christian School
Elkhart Cyber School
Futures International High School
Michigan Virtual High School
The Potter's School
Virtual High School
Anatomy/Physiology
American Virtual High School
Ancient Astronomy
Abaetern Academy
Animal Behavior and Zoology
Virtual High School
Animal Health
Intelligent Education
Astronomy
Abaetern Academy
Colorado Online Learning
Evergreen Internet Academy
Intelligent Education
Louisiana Virtual School
Michigan Virtual High School
Monroe Virtual High School
Northern Star Online
On Line Academy
PA LEARNERS Online Regional
 Cyber Charter School
Scholars' Online Academy
TRECA Digital Academy
Virtual High School
Virtual High School@PWCS
Astronomy (Honors)
Intelligent Education
West Virginia Virtual School
Astronomy and Space
Futures International High School

University of Nebraska-Lincoln
Independent Study High School
University of Oklahoma High School
USA International On-Line School
Vilas eSchool
Virtual Community School of Ohio
Warren County Virtual Community
School
Wichita eSchool

Biology 1
Clark County School District Virtual
High School
Cumberland County Schools' Web
Academy
Delta Cyber School
Evergreen Internet Academy
Fairfax County Public Schools
Online Campus
Georgia Virtual School
Illinois Virtual High School
Indiana University High School
Internet High School
Louisiana Virtual School
Monroe Virtual High School
On Line Academy
Portland State University
Independent Study
Texas Tech University Extended
Studies
University of Texas at Austin High
School
Vilas eSchool
Virtual Greenbush
Virtual High School@PWCS
Westside Virtual High School
York County School Division Virtual
High School

Biology 1 Honors
Clark County School District Virtual
High School
Monroe Virtual High School

Biology 10
Colorado State Academy

Biology 2
Evergreen Internet Academy
Louisiana Virtual School
Monroe Virtual High School
On Line Academy
Portland State University
Independent Study

Biology 2A Anatomy/Physiology
Primavera Online High School

Biology 2A Botany/Zoology
Primavera Online High School

Biology Honors
Center for Talent Development
Warren County Virtual Community
School

Biology Lab
Babbage Net School
James Madison High School Online

Biology with Lab
Warren County Virtual Community
School

Biology with Lab Honors
Warren County Virtual Community
School

Biotechnology
Illinois Virtual High School
Virtual High School

Black Holes
Abaetern Academy

Botany
Delta Cyber School

Chemistry
Alabama Online High School
Alpha Omega Academy
American Virtual High School
Babbage Net School
Blueprint Education
Choice 2000 Online High School
Christa McAuliffe Academy
CompuHigh/Whitmore School
Delta Cyber School
Eagle Christian School
Eldorado Academy

College Physics
Colorado Online Learning
College Preparatory Biology
Gwinnett County Online Campus
College Preparatory Chemistry
Gwinnett County Online Campus
College Preparatory Physics
Gwinnett County Online Campus
Concepts in Physical Science
SK Online
Conceptual Physics
Abaetern Academy
Evergreen Internet Academy
Louisiana Virtual School
Missouri Virtual School
**Conservation of Our Natural
Resources**
Monroe Virtual High School
Pennsylvania Cyber Charter School
University of Missouri-Columbia
High School
Crop Science
Intelligent Education
Disease and Disorders
Eldorado Academy
DNA Technology
Virtual High School
Earth and Space
Karval Online Education
Earth and Space Science
Kentucky Virtual High School
Primavera Online High School
Earth Science
3D Learn
American Virtual High School
Babbage Net School
Basehor-Linwood Virtual School
Blueprint Education
Central Connecticut Adventist
Virtual School
Choice 2000 Online High School
Christa McAuliffe Academy
Clintondale Virtual High School

Delta Cyber School
Eldorado Academy
Futures International High School
iQ Academies
Keystone National High School
Laurel Springs School
Louisiana Virtual School
Michigan Virtual High School
Minnesota Online High School
On Line Academy
PA LEARNERS Online Regional
Cyber Charter School
Pennsylvania Cyber Charter School
Pinnacle Education Virtual School
Providence High School
SK Online
Trent High School
Virtual Community School of Ohio
Virtual High School@PWCS
Warren County Virtual Community
School
York County School Division Virtual
High School
Earth Science 1
Internet Academy
Portland State University
Independent Study
Earth Science 2
Portland State University
Independent Study
Earth Science Honors
Laurel Springs School
Warren County Virtual Community
School
Earth Systems
Electronic High School
Earth/Space Science
Christa McAuliffe Academy
Florida Virtual School
Stetson University Virtual School
University of Miami Online High
School
USA International On-Line School
Wichita eSchool

Food and Science
Electronic High School

Foods and Nutrition
Monroe Virtual High School
University of Missouri-Columbia
High School

Fundamentals in Science
Colorado Online Learning

Fundamentals of Chemistry
Missouri Virtual School

Fundamentals of Technology
Cumberland County Schools' Web
Academy

Future Issues: Biotechnology
Colorado Online Learning

General Biology
Pennsylvania Cyber Charter School
SK Online

General Biology 1
Cyber Oregon Online COOLSchool

General Science
Blueprint Education
Delta Cyber School
Elkhart Cyber School
Laurel Springs School
Sycamore Academy
Vilas eSchool
Warren County Virtual Community
School

Genetics
Intelligent Education

Geology
American Virtual High School
Colorado Online Learning
Evergreen Internet Academy
Houston Independent School District
Virtual School
Illinois Virtual High School
Intelligent Education

Geology Honors
Intelligent Education

Geosystems
Fairfax County Public Schools
Online Campus

**Germs and Disease: The Inheritance
of Human Genetic Disorders**
Virtual High School

Gravity and Relativity
Abaetern Academy

**Great Inventions and Scientific
Discoveries**
Virtual High School

Health/Anatomy and Physiology
Oak Meadow School

Honors Biology
Florida Virtual School
Keystone National High School
Laurel Springs School
Stetson University Virtual School
University of Miami Online High
School
USA International On-Line School

Human Anatomy and Physiology
Intelligent Education
On Line Academy

Human Biology
Electronic High School

Human Space Exploration
Michigan Virtual High School

Integrated Physics and Chemistry
Houston Independent School District
Virtual School
University of Texas at Austin High
School

Introduction to Animal Biology
Intelligent Education

Introduction to Astronomy
The Potter's School
University of Oklahoma High School
Virtual High School

Introduction to Aviation Science
University of Oklahoma High School

Introduction to Biology
American Virtual High School

Marine Science Honors
Florida Virtual School
Stetson University Virtual School

Mechanics in Physics
Virtual High School

Meteorology
Intelligent Education
Virtual High School

Modern Earth Science
Intelligent Education

Motion and Forces
Abaetern Academy

Mysteries of the Solar System
Pennsylvania Cyber Charter School

NASA
Delta Cyber School

Natural History of Oregon Country
Cyber Oregon Online COOLSchool

The Night Sky
Abaetern Academy

Nuclear Physics
Virtual High School

Oceanography
Delta Cyber School
Illinois Virtual High School
Laurel Springs School
Michigan Virtual High School
PA LEARNERS Online Regional
    Cyber Charter School
Plano ISD eSchool
QualitySchoolHouse
Virtual Greenbush
Warren County Virtual Community
    School
West Virginia Virtual School

Oceanography (Honors)
West Virginia Virtual School

Oceanography Honors
Intelligent Education
Laurel Springs School
Warren County Virtual Community
    School

Particle Physics
Abaetern Academy

Physical Science
3D Learn
Alabama Online High School
Alpha Omega Academy
Babbage Net School
Basehor-Linwood Virtual School
Choice 2000 Online High School
Christa McAuliffe Academy
Clintondale Virtual High School
Cumberland County Schools' Web
    Academy
Delta Cyber School
Eagle Christian School
Eldorado Academy
Futures International High School
Georgia Virtual School
Intelligent Education
Internet Academy
Keystone National High School
Minnesota Center of Online Learning
Monroe Virtual High School
North Dakota Division of
    Independent Study
On Line Academy
Oregon Online
PA LEARNERS Online Regional
    Cyber Charter School
Pennsylvania Cyber Charter School
Pinnacle Education Virtual School
Providence High School
University of Missouri-Columbia
    High School
University of Nebraska-Lincoln
    Independent Study High School
University of Oklahoma High School
Virtual Community School of Ohio

Physical Science 1
Evergreen Internet Academy

Physical Science 2
Evergreen Internet Academy

Physical Science Lab
James Madison High School Online

Physics 12
Colorado State Academy

Physics 2
Kentucky Virtual High School
Monroe Virtual High School

Physics C – Mechanics
Education Program for Gifted Youth

Physics C: Electricity and Magnetism
Education Program for Gifted Youth

Physics Honors
Florida Virtual School
Kentucky Virtual High School
Stetson University Virtual School
UC College Prep Online

Physics Lab
James Madison High School Online

Physics with Lab
Warren County Virtual Community School

Physics with Lab Honors
Warren County Virtual Community School

Physiology and Anatomy
South Dakota Virtual Campus

Pre-A.P. Biology
Virtual High School

Pre-A.P. Chemistry
Virtual High School

Pre-A.P. Enviromental Science
Virtual High School

Pre-A.P. Physics B
Virtual High School

Pre-Engineering Technology
Electronic High School

Principles of Biological Science
Missouri Virtual School

Principles of Biology
Primavera Online High School

Principles of Science
Clark County School District Virtual High School

Principles of Technology
Electronic High School

Resources of the Earth
Intelligent Education

Resources of the Earth Honors
Intelligent Education

Science 10
NorthStar Academy

Science 9
NorthStar Academy
Northern Star Online

Science Inquiry
PA LEARNERS Online Regional Cyber Charter School

Science Research Seminar
On Line Academy

Special Needs – Integrated Science
Warren County Virtual Community School

Special Topics in Geology
Monroe Virtual High School
Pennsylvania Cyber Charter School

Study of the Environment
Laurel Springs School
Warren County Virtual Community School

Studying Planet Earth
Monroe Virtual High School
Pennsylvania Cyber Charter School
University of Missouri-Columbia High School

The Sun
Abaetern Academy

Technical Chemistry
Gwinnett County Online Campus

Technical Physics
Gwinnett County Online Campus

Technology of Machine Tools
Intelligent Education

Thermodynamics
Abaetern Academy

The Underground World of Caves
Monroe Virtual High School

Stetson University Virtual School
UC College Prep Online
Virtual Advanced Placement School
Virtual High School
West Virginia Virtual School

A.P. Psychology
Center for Talent Development
Clark County School District Virtual
High School
Fairfax County Public Schools
Online Campus
Georgia Virtual School
Gwinnett County Online Campus
Illinois Virtual High School
Intelligent Education
Kentucky Virtual High School
Michigan Virtual High School
National University Virtual High
School
Texas Virtual School
Virtual Advanced Placement School
West Virginia Virtual School

A.P. U.S. Government
Florida Virtual School
Georgia Virtual School
Maryland Virtual Learning
Opportunities
Mississippi Online Learning Institute
University of Miami Online High
School
University of Oklahoma High School

A.P. U.S. Government and Politics
Clark County School District Virtual
High School
Fairfax County Public Schools
Online Campus
Illinois Virtual High School
Kentucky Virtual High School
Michigan Virtual High School
Missouri Virtual School
Stetson University Virtual School
Texas Virtual School
UC College Prep Online

Virtual Advanced Placement School
West Virginia Virtual School

A.P. U.S. History
Florida Virtual School
Kentucky Virtual High School

Adult U.S. Constitution
Colorado State Academy

American Civics
Intelligent Education

American Foreign Policy
Virtual High School

American Government
American Virtual High School
Babbage Net School
Blueprint Education
CompuHigh/Whitmore School
Cyber Oregon Online COOLSchool
Florida Virtual School
The Francis School
Futures International High School
Georgia Virtual School
Intelligent Education
iQ Academies
James Madison High School Online
Keystone National High School
Michigan Virtual High School
Minnesota Center of Online Learning
Mississippi Online Learning Institute
Monroe Virtual High School
National University Virtual High
School
North Dakota Division of
Independent Study
PA LEARNERS Online Regional
Cyber Charter School
Pennsylvania Cyber Charter School
Pinnacle Education Virtual School
Plano ISD eSchool
Providence High School
QualitySchoolHouse
Regina Coeli Academy
SK Online
Stetson University Virtual School

Monroe Virtual High School
PA LEARNERS Online Regional
Cyber Charter School
Pennsylvania Cyber Charter School
South Dakota Virtual Campus
University of Nebraska-Lincoln
Independent Study High School
Virtual Greenbush
West Virginia Virtual School
Westside Virtual High School

Civics and Economics
Cumberland County Schools' Web
Academy

Civics and Economics Honors
Cumberland County Schools' Web
Academy

Civics Honors
Keystone National High School

Civics in Cyberspace
Illinois Virtual High School

Civics/Citizenship
Georgia Virtual School

Civil Liberties
Clark County School District Virtual
High School

College Preparatory Economics
Gwinnett County Online Campus

**College Preparatory Political
Systems**
Gwinnett County Online Campus

**College Preparatory World
Geography**
Gwinnett County Online Campus

Comparative Politics
Monroe Virtual High School
Pennsylvania Cyber Charter School

Contemporary Issues
3D Learn
Basehor-Linwood Virtual School

Contemporary Problems
Clark County School District Virtual
High School

Controversial Issues
Gwinnett County Online Campus

Corrections in the 21st Century
Intelligent Education

Crime and Justice
Clark County School District Virtual
High School

Criminal Evidence
Intelligent Education

Criminal Investigation
Intelligent Education

Criminal Justice
3D Learn
Intelligent Education

Criminal Justice 1
Cumberland County Schools' Web
Academy

**Critical Thinking Honors: Informal
Logic**
Center for Talent Development

**Critical Thinking Honors: Mass
Media**
Center for Talent Development

Cultural Anthropology
Intelligent Education

Cultural Anthropology Honors
Intelligent Education

Cultural Geography
Futures International High School

**Cultural Identity Through
Literature**
Virtual High School

Current Events
Abaetern Academy
North Dakota Division of
Independent Study

Current Issues
Portland State University
Independent Study

Current World Affairs
South Dakota Virtual Campus

Democracy in America?
Virtual High School

General Sociology
Portland State University
Independent Study

Geography
Babbage Net School
iQ Academies
Keystone National High School
Michigan Virtual High School
PA LEARNERS Online Regional
Cyber Charter School
The Potter's School
SK Online
TRECA Digital Academy
USA International On-Line School
Vilas eSchool
West Virginia Virtual School

Geography and Modern World History
Eldorado Academy

Geography for Life
Electronic High School

Geography Honors
Keystone National High School

Geopolitical Economics
Clark County School District Virtual High School

Ghoulies, Ghosties, and Long-Legged Beasties: Why We Like to be Scared
Virtual High School

Global Issues
Michigan Virtual High School
SK Online

Global Politics
North Dakota Division of Independent Study

Global Studies
Florida Virtual School
Monroe Virtual High School
Stetson University Virtual School
USA International On-Line School
West Virginia Virtual School

Global Studies 1
Portland State University
Independent Study

Global Studies 2
Portland State University
Independent Study

Gods of CNN: The Power of Modern Media
Virtual High School

Government
Clintondale Virtual High School
Karval Online Education
Minnesota Online High School
Portland State University
Independent Study
Sycamore Academy
Wichita eSchool

Government 9
Northern Star Online

Government and Economics
Alpha Omega Academy
Eagle Christian School
The Grace Academy
The Jubilee Academy
The MorningStar Academy

Government and the Constitution
The Potter's School

Government/Geography 9
Colorado State Academy

Honors Economics
Florida Virtual School
Keystone National High School
Stetson University Virtual School
University of Miami Online High School

Human Growth and Development
Intelligent Education

Identity
Abaetern Academy

International Studies
OSU K–12 Online

Introduction to Child Development
Northern Star Online

Principles of Economics
  Portland State University
    Independent Study
Problems of Democracy
  3D Learn
Psychology
  American Virtual High School
  Babbage Net School
  Basehor-Linwood Virtual School
  Cumberland County Schools' Web
    Academy
  Eldorado Academy
  Electronic High School
  Futures International High School
  Georgia Virtual School
  Gwinnett County Online Campus
  Illinois Virtual High School
  Intelligent Education
  Internet Academy
  iQ Academies
  James Madison High School Online
  Keystone National High School
  Michigan Virtual High School
  Mississippi Online Learning Institute
  Monroe Virtual High School
  Oak Meadow School
  PA LEARNERS Online Regional
    Cyber Charter School
  Pennsylvania Cyber Charter School
  Plano ISD eSchool
  SK Online
  TRECA Digital Academy
  University of Miami Online High
    School
  University of Nebraska-Lincoln
    Independent Study High School
  Vilas eSchool
  Virtual Community School of Ohio
  Virtual Greenbush
  West Virginia Virtual School
  Westside Virtual High School
  York County School Division Virtual
    High School

Psychology – An Introduction
  Virtual High School
Psychology — Training
  Mississippi Online Learning Institute
Psychology 1
  Clark County School District Virtual
    High School
  Cyber Oregon Online COOLSchool
Psychology Honors
  Center for Talent Development
  UC College Prep Online
Psychology/Sociology
  Elkhart Cyber School
Religions of the World
  Blueprint Education
Seasons
  Abaetern Academy
Senior Economics
  SK Online
**Social Issues in a Contemporary
World**
  Monroe Virtual High School
  Pennsylvania Cyber Charter School
Social Studies on the Web
  Cyber Oregon Online COOLSchool
Social Studies/Geography
  Alpha Omega Academy
Sociology
  American Virtual High School
  Babbage Net School
  Basehor-Linwood Virtual School
  Cumberland County Schools' Web
    Academy
  Eldorado Academy
  Electronic High School
  Futures International High School
  Gwinnett County Online Campus
  Intelligent Education
  Keystone National High School
  Michigan Virtual High School
  Monroe Virtual High School
  North Dakota Division of
    Independent Study

World Civilizations
Illinois Virtual High School
iQ Academies
Michigan Virtual High School
Minnesota Center of Online Learning
PA LEARNERS Online Regional
 Cyber Charter School
Westside Virtual High School

**World Conflict, a United Nations
Introduction**
Virtual High School

World Culture
Abaetern Academy

World Cultures
Laurel Springs School
Monroe Virtual High School
Oregon Online
University of Nebraska-Lincoln
 Independent Study High School
Warren County Virtual Community
 School

World Geography
American Virtual High School
Blueprint Education
Choice 2000 Online High School
Clintondale Virtual High School
Colorado Online Learning
CompuHigh/Whitmore School
Cumberland County Schools' Web
 Academy
Cyber Oregon Online COOLSchool
Delta Cyber School
Electronic High School
Elkhart Cyber School
Georgia Virtual School
Houston Independent School District
 Virtual School
Intelligent Education
Karval Online Education
Monroe Virtual High School
North Dakota Division of
 Independent Study
NorthStar Academy

Plano ISD eSchool
Providence High School
QualitySchoolHouse
South Dakota Virtual Campus
Sycamore Academy
University of Missouri-Columbia
 High School
University of Nebraska-Lincoln
 Independent Study High School
University of Oklahoma High School
Virtual High School@PWCS
York County School Division Virtual
 High School

World Geography Studies
Texas Tech University Extended
 Studies
University of Texas at Austin High
 School

World Geography/History
Blueprint Education

World Mythology
Intelligent Education

The World of Geography
The Potter's School

World Perspectives Honors
Center for Talent Development

World Religions
The Grace Academy
The Jubilee Academy
Monroe Virtual High School
The MorningStar Academy
Pennsylvania Cyber Charter School
The Potter's School
University of Missouri-Columbia
 High School

World Studies
Eagle Christian School
Northern Star Online

The World Today
Abaetern Academy

World View in Conflict
NorthStar Academy

Careers
Vilas eSchool

Character Education
North Dakota Division of
Independent Study

Child Care
Basehor-Linwood Virtual School

Child Care Management
American Virtual High School

The Child Care Professional
Intelligent Education

Clothing and Textiles
Monroe Virtual High School
Pennsylvania Cyber Charter School

**College Awareness and Career
Preparation**
OSU K–12 Online

College Planner
Sycamore Academy

College Preparation
NorthStar Academy

College Survival
Clark County School District Virtual
High School

Community Service
Choice 2000 Online High School
CompuHigh/Whitmore School

Computer-Based Study Strategies
Cyber Oregon Online COOLSchool

Consumer Economics
Monroe Virtual High School
On Line Academy
Pennsylvania Cyber Charter School
University of Missouri-Columbia
High School

Consumer Education
Clark County School District Virtual
High School
Illinois Virtual High School

**Consumer Education and
Economics**
Monroe Virtual High School

University of Nebraska-Lincoln
Independent Study High School

Consumer Finance
OSU K–12 Online

Consumer Science 1
Vilas eSchool

Consumer Science 2
Vilas eSchool

Contemporary Living
Futures International High School

Critical Thinking
Monroe Virtual High School
Pennsylvania Cyber Charter School

Cyber Study Skills
Cyber Oregon Online COOLSchool

Dating, Marriage, and Family
OSU K–12 Online

Diversified Work Experience
Blueprint Education

Drafting
Cumberland County Schools' Web
Academy

Effective Methods of Study
Monroe Virtual High School
University of Nebraska-Lincoln
Independent Study High School

Emotional Intelligence
Northern Star Online

Employability Skills
Michigan Virtual High School
Virtual High School

Etiquette: Manners for Today
University of Oklahoma High School

Exam Review
Michigan Virtual High School

Family and Personal Etiquette
Monroe Virtual High School
University of Nebraska-Lincoln
Independent Study High School

FCAT Prep
Florida Virtual School

Financial Literacy
Electronic High School

Life and Job Skills
Michigan Virtual High School

Life Management
Blueprint Education
Cumberland County Schools' Web
  Academy
Laurel Springs School
Warren County Virtual Community
  School

Life Management Skills
Cyber Oregon Online COOLSchool
Florida Virtual School
Monroe Virtual High School
Stetson University Virtual School
USA International On-Line School
Virtual Greenbush

Life Planning
York County School Division Virtual
  High School

Life Skills
The Grace Academy
The Jubilee Academy
The MorningStar Academy
Virtual Community School of Ohio

**Living, Learning, and Earning:
Consumer Economics**
Kentucky Virtual High School

MEAP Smart Curriculum
Michigan Virtual High School

Motorcycle Repair
Intelligent Education

Occupational Ed
Christa McAuliffe Academy

Parenting
Blueprint Education
Intelligent Education
Vilas eSchool

**Parenting in the Twenty-First
Century**
Virtual High School

Peacemaking
Virtual High School

**Personal Adjustment and Family
Living**
Monroe Virtual High School
University of Nebraska-Lincoln
  Independent Study High School

**Personal Adjustment, Dating, and
Marriage**
Monroe Virtual High School
Pennsylvania Cyber Charter School

Personal and Family Development
Texas Tech University Extended
  Studies

Personal and Family Living
PA LEARNERS Online Regional
  Cyber Charter School

**Personal and Interpersonal
Development**
Illinois Virtual High School

Personal Economics and Finance
Illinois Virtual High School
iQ Academies
Karval Online Education
Michigan Virtual High School
Minnesota Center of Online Learning
Mississippi Online Learning Institute
PA LEARNERS Online Regional
  Cyber Charter School
Virtual Greenbush
West Virginia Virtual School
Westside Virtual High School

Personal Enhancement
SK Online

Personal Finance
Cyber Oregon Online COOLSchool
Indiana University High School
Internet Academy
Monroe Virtual High School
North Dakota Division of
  Independent Study
Oregon Online
Virtual High School
York County School Division Virtual
  High School

University of Nebraska-Lincoln
  Independent Study High School
Small-Engine Maintenance and Repair
  Monroe Virtual High School
  University of Nebraska-Lincoln
    Independent Study High School
Stress Management
  American Virtual High School
  CompuHigh/Whitmore School
Study Skills
  Blueprint Education
  Clark County School District Virtual
    High School
  Michigan Virtual High School
  PA LEARNERS Online Regional
    Cyber Charter School
  Plano ISD eSchool
  TRECA Digital Academy
  West Virginia Virtual School
  Westside Virtual High School
Study Skills 1
  Karval Online Education
Study Skills: Learning Fundamentals
  Illinois Virtual High School
  Virtual Greenbush
Studying in College and Other Places
  Monroe Virtual High School
Success
  Internet Academy
Success 101
  Cumberland County Schools' Web
    Academy
SuperStructures
  Virtual Greenbush
Technical Careers Exploration
  Northern Star Online
Teen and Family Living
  University of Missouri-Columbia
    High School

Test Preparation
  Georgia Virtual School
Think About It
  CompuHigh/Whitmore School
Thinking and Learning Strategies
  Florida Virtual School
  Stetson University Virtual School
Understanding and Improving Your Memory
  Indiana University High School
  Monroe Virtual High School
Vocational Experience
  Colorado State Academy
Vocational Information
  Monroe Virtual High School
Voluntary Community Service
  University of Miami Online High
    School
Work Experience
  Choice 2000 Online High School
Work-Study
  On Line Academy
Work-Study Program
  Vilas eSchool
World of Work
  Pinnacle Education Virtual School
Your Employment Success
  Blueprint Education

Geographical Index

The following index lists online high schools by state. This index may be helpful if you are looking for a public institution in your own state that offers free or reduced tuition to the state's residents or if you are looking for courses that conform to a specific state's educational requirements.

Alabama
Alabama Online High School

Alaska
Delta Cyber School
QualitySchoolHouse
SeeUOnline

Arizona
Alpha Omega Academy
Blueprint Education
Internet Home School
Pinnacle Education Virtual School
Primavera Online High School
Regina Coeli Academy
Scholars' Online Academy

California
Choice 2000 Online High School
Dennison Online Internet School
Education Program for Gifted Youth
Futures International High School
Laurel Springs School
National University Virtual High
    School
Sycamore Academy
UC College Prep Online

Colorado
Colorado Online Learning
Colorado State Academy
Eldorado Academy
JeffcoNet Academy
Karval Online Education
NorthStar Academy
On Line Academy
USA International Online School
Vilas eSchool

Connecticut
Central Connecticut Adventist
    Virtual School

Florida
3D Learn
American Virtual High School
Florida Virtual School
The MorningStar Academy
Stetson University Virtual School
University of Miami Online High
    School

Georgia
Georgia Virtual School
Gwinnett County Online Campus
Intelligent Education
James Madison High School Online

Hawaii
E-School

Illinois
Center for Talent Development
Illinois Virtual High School
The Jubilee Academy

Indiana
Indiana University High School

Kansas
Basehor-Linwood Virtual School
Elkhart Cyber School
Virtual Greenbush
Wichita eSchool

Kentucky
Kentucky Virtual High School
Providence High School

Louisiana
Louisiana Virtual School

Maryland
Maryland Virtual Learning
    Opportunities

Massachusetts
Virtual High School

Virginia
Fairfax County Public Schools
   Online Campus
Internet High School
The Potter's School
Virginia Satellite Educational
   Network
Virtual Advanced Placement School
Virtual High School@PWCS
York County School Division Virtual
   High School

Washington State
Christa McAuliffe Academy
Evergreen Internet Academy
Internet Academy

West Virginia
CompuHigh/Whitmore School
West Virginia Virtual School

Wisconsin
iQ Academies
Milwaukee Area Technical College
Monroe Virtual High School
Victory Math